MW00981929

OSHO
Fragrance

OSHO
Fragrance

SWAMI CHAITANYA KEERTI

wisdom
tree

© Swami Chaitanya Keerti, 2005
First published 2005
Reprinted 2006, 2008, 2011, 2013

ISBN: 978-81-8328-003-7

All rights reserved. No part of this book may be reproduced, stored in a retrieval system or transmitted in any form or by any means — electronic, mechanical, photocopying, recording or otherwise — without the prior permission of the author and the publisher.

Published by
Wisdom Tree
4779/23, Ansari Road
Darya Ganj, New Delhi-110002
Ph.: 23247966/67/68
wisdomtreebooks@gmail.com

Printed in India

Preface

O*sho Fragrance* is a compilation of Swami Chaitanya Keerti's
aricles already published in various newspapers during
the last two years. Special thanks go to Ma Prem Naina who
diligently tracked them in the dailies through 2003-04. Although
hundreds of thousands of people have already read these articles,
we are all aware that the life of daily newspapers is not
beyond one day. To impart longevity to these precious articles,
they have been compiled in this book. Inspired by Osho's
insights, these articles carry his message of timelessness even
though written over a certain period of time. As this
compilation carries fragrance of Osho's wisdom, hence the
title *Osho Fragrance*.

As a disciple of Osho, Swami Chaitanya Keerti has been
spreading his master's message for over three decades. Initiated
by Osho into neo-*sannyas*, he has been fully involved in this
play that he treats not as work. He began by travelling to
various Indian cities, singing and dancing on the streets in
kirtan groups. Two years later, he started editing and publishing
Osho's magazine from Ludhiana, Punjab.

In 1974, Osho invited him to his *ahsram* to be editor of the
Rajneesh Foundation Newsletter, which is known today as *Osho*

Times International and is published from Pune. Since May 2001, he has been editing the *Osho World* magazine in Hindi, and now also in English, published by Osho World Foundation, New Delhi. In accordance with his master's message, he has been quoting from Osho's discourses and has contributed articles to several publications.

True to his intention, I am sure this fragrant compilation will inspire you to further read and listen to the words of his master available in over 600 books, and to infuse his message, which is beyond words.

11 December, 2004   **Ma Shashin**

Contents

The Self

And if your meditation starts blossoming you will not have any other birth in the body. You will simply disappear, like incense disappearing into the blue sky, or fragrance of roses disappearing into the blue sky. You will become part of the cosmos.

—Osho

Radiate Positive Vibrations

Every human being who is really alive is constantly broadcasting thoughts, feelings and vibrations, even if one sits in silence. The very presence of a person is communicative and radiates bioelectric waves or vibrations around and these affect whatever is surrounding him. Every person carries his atmosphere wherever one goes or lives. You go to a person and sit in his presence and suddenly you feel very happy and cheerful. Quite the contrary may happen in the presence of another person: You may become sad or depressed or feel that your energy has been sucked. And with another type of person, you may not feel anything, just a deadness.

Meditation is a conscious effort to become fully alive and radiate positive vibrations. A meditative person is a joy to be with. You feel uplifted in his presence and a certain kind of relaxation, rejuvenation and rejoicing enters your being.

Your *prana* (energy) feels expansion. It is not some kind of imagination or hallucination; it actually happens, and sensitive people can experience it. So it is very important for you to see with whom you relate or spend your time with. A sensitive person will choose the company of people carefully, because this life is precious.

OSHO FRAGRANCE

Osho advised all to fill one's life with love. Practise love. Sitting alone in your room, be loving. Radiate love. Fill the whole room with your love energy. Feel vibrating with a new frequency, feel swaying as if you are in the ocean of love. Create vibrations of love energy around you. And you will start feeling immediately that something is happening — something in your aura is changing, something around your body is changing; a warmth is arising around your body.... You are becoming more alive. Something like sleep is disappearing. Something like awareness is arising. Sway into this ocean. Dance, sing and let your whole room be filled with love.

Love that depends on somebody is a poor love. Love that is created within you, love that you create out of your own being is real energy.

3

Knowing Oneself can Lead to God

Osho tells a beautiful story from the *Upanishads*. Once a young man, Shwetaketu, came back from his Gurukul, the family of his guru, learned, and very proud of his learning. His father, the seer Uddalak, watched him coming and became sad. 'This is not learning! Here comes the son so proud and haughty, he must have become a man of knowledge,' he thought. The son came and touched his father's feet but it was a mere formality. How can a man who has become so egoistic bow down?

The father said, "Shwetaketu, I see your body bent, but not you. And what misfortune has happened to you? Why do you look so haughty? A man of knowing becomes humble. Have you heard anything about that One, knowing which, one knows all?"

Shwetaketu replied: "What are you talking about? How can one know all by knowing One? Absurd! I have known all that could be known in the university. I have become as profound as one can become in all the subjects that are taught there. When my master said to me: 'Now you know all and you can go back home,' only then did I return. But I have never heard of 'One'. How can one know all by knowing One?"

Uddalak said, "Yes, that One is you. *Tat twam asi*, that art thou. If you know this One you will know all. You have wasted your energy. Go back! Never come again unless you know that One by knowing which all is known, because in our family no one has been a Brahmin just by name. We have called ourselves Brahmins because we have known the Brahma. You don't belong to our family if you don't know that One; go back!"

Shwetaketu returned to the university again and returned after 10 to 12 years. The moment his father saw him coming, he ran out of the back door. His wife asked, "Where are you going? Your son is coming."

He replied, "I cannot face him; moreover, I cannot allow him to touch my feet; it will look awkward. He has really become a Brahmin. He now knows the Brahma. Brahma is the ultimate life source. I am only a Brahmin by birth but he has earned it. If he does not touch my feet, that will look awkward, if he does touch my feet, that will look awkward, if I touch his feet that too will look awkward. So it is better that I escape. I will return only when I am also a Brahmin by my own realisation."

Still Your Inner Self to Control Your Actions

Violence is an effect, an outward manifestation. So is anger, so is all evil. A man hoards money or indulges in adulteration. These are merely consequences. We want to do with a particular result, without understanding the cause. As long as the cause is there, the effect is bound to follow. If the root is not dissolved, the result flowing therefrom would remain. Anger doesn't happen on its own; behind it lies a particular disposition, and behind that the fundamental nature of the person concerned. The inner overcomes the outer: We cannot remove outward evil without bringing about a fundamental inner transformation.

Psychologists have analysed man's essential nature. A particular nature gives rise to certain tendencies with certain consequences. All scriptures, too, speak not of mere outward change, but deep inner transformation. I have also posed this question before would-be ascetics — those who want to renounce family and home to become ascetics. "Is it possible," I asked, "to achieve non-violence or continence or non-acquisitiveness through an effort of will?"

They say it can be done. We exercise our will. Well, I resolve to do or not to do something. I take a vow, for example, not to tell a lie. But is that any guarantee that I will no more tell lies, or give way to anger? If one could ensure non-violence through mere exertion of one's will, it would be wonderful. One could resolve to remove a particular evil, but mere resolution does not end it. It would be wonderful if the mere utterance of a word could accomplish results.

Religious mystics have offered a way — the disciplining of the mind, body and tongue. With discipline comes fulfillment. If the mind is still, non-violence comes into being. If the mind is pure and still, continence follows; also non-greed. But if the mind is restless, if it wanders like a monkey, if it runs after various objects, preoccupied with persons and things, how can there be non-violence or continence? Behaving like a monkey would not bring it forth. If it were so simple, I would urge the whole world to take to the monastic life; none should remain outside the fold. Just pronounce a word and the thing, whatever it is, is done! But in reality it is not so. And a spiritual practitioner who tries to go forward without first maturing his meditation, is often obliged to retrace his steps.

One Needs to be at Home with Oneself

J. Krishnamurti, the enlightened mystic, once said: "We gossip about others because we are not sufficiently interested in the process of our own thinking and our own action."

The average human being does not live more than 60 to 70 years, and what does he do during these years? Most of the time he spends gossiping, thinking and worrying about things that really don't concern him directly, and he is left with little time to do something for his own life.

Life is really very precious and if we were to realise this, we would have no time for petty things. Instead, we would utilise our time in raising our own consciousness.

The Russian mystic, Gurdjieff used to say: "We live in such a sleepy state of consciousness that if we really count the minutes we spend when we are really aware, fully conscious, it will be not more than five minutes in all the 60 years. Out of this, 20 years are spent in sleeping. While the rest of the 40 years are spent in day-dreaming, fulfilling our ambitions and desires, and chasing mirages. And in the end we find really nothing in our hands."

In order to make his point, Gurdjieff gave an example. He

said that we cannot concentrate for 60 seconds on the movement of seconds by our wrist-watch — our mind will wander away quickly. "It may take three months to accomplish this much concentration. This is the state of our consciousness — always in turmoil. And having such a disturbed state of mind, we cannot truly celebrate our life. We are not really home; we are not there in our mind where we are physically. Mind is all ripples and our being is not visible in totality in these ripples. Meditation takes us beyond these ripples, and there we are at home."

9

Device of Transforming Emotions

Gurdjieff, a Russian mystic, was a great enlightened master of the modern times. Though he was not educated, he had several intellectual disciples, such as P. D. Auspensky and Catherine Mansfield. Often the disciples found it hard to work with him even though they were intelligent.

He would create situations to arouse all kinds of emotions in the disciples and they were asked to face the emotions. He would create a situation where a new person would lose his/her temper, without realising that Gurdjieff had created the situation.

Osho called it a group device.

Such situations can be created, but only in a school where many people are working on themselves. And when Gurdjieff would shout, "Remember! Remain undisturbed," one would immediately know that this was a 'created' situation. The disturbance cannot disappear so suddenly because it has physical roots.

Osho explained: "Anger cannot disappear so immediately. Even now that you had come to know that you had been deceived, that no one was insulting you and no one meant anything by it, it would be difficult to do anything. The anger is there, your body is filled with it — but suddenly your temperature cools down. The anger remains only on the body. At the centre you cool down, and you know that a point exists within you which is undisturbed. You start laughing. Your eyes are red with anger, your face is violent, but you start laughing. You know two things — a point which is undisturbed and a periphery which is disturbed."

Body is Divine

"I am in tremendous love with life, hence I teach celebration. Everything has to be celebrated, everything has to be lived, loved. To me nothing is mundane and nothing is sacred. To me all is sacred — from the lowest rung of the ladder to the highest rung. It is the same ladder: From the body to the soul, from the physical to the spiritual, from sex to *samadhi* — everything is divine!" Osho: Come. Come, Yet Again Come.

Ecstasy exists on many levels. The body is the first level. If we have not known ecstasy on the physical level, it is doubtful that we will know any ecstasy on deeper levels of the heart and soul. One has to start from the beginning. The body is the first step on the inner journey. Every child knows bodily ecstasy by instinct and enjoys it unless and until parents and the society start teaching him the condemnation of his or her natural instincts. The child begins to understand that there's something in him or her that is not acceptable. And then begins the journey of being unnatural.

The more civilised the family the more unnatural it tends to become. The further one goes from nature the more pervert one becomes.

Most of our illnesses are rooted in our unnatural lifestyles. All our neurosis and schizophrenia is the result of not living naturally — not living in harmony within ourselves, not accepting our instincts in their purity. The first and foremost step on the path of meditation is to accept our body, feel our senses and become aware of them in their entireness. We should not create any split between the body and soul. In reality they are one. The body is the manifestation of soul and the soul is the invisible body. They are inter-dependent. Can the soul exist without the body? It may. But how would you know it! Can the body be alive without the soul?

No. The body needs the soul to breathe and throb. They exist together as an indivisible organic unity. This is the meaning of yoga. There is no real duality between the body and soul as they exist together in Advaita. Only in ignorance we do not recognise Advaita. This attitude towards our body gives us the right kind of attitude about how to behave with our body. We feel something of the divine in our body and stop mistreating it. If we consider our body a temple of the divine, it becomes impossible to misbehave with it or keep it unclean. We know then that this temple has to be kept always clean. Then there is no question of any indulgence in wrong and unhealthy things. The feeling and remembrance of a temple, the sacredness itself will make it difficult for us to do anything ugly to our body.

The trouble is that most of us are not taught to feel this way. Generally we are taught to look at our body as something sinful — an abode of all kinds of sins. And for this our religions which are dominated by puritan priests and rigid morality-preachers are responsible. In the beginning they impose unnatural condemnation from outside and later it becomes an inseparable part of our conditioning.

So the first thing is to drop all this body condemnation and become natural. Have love and respect for it. Feel it from within as if you are entering the temple of the divine, which it is, because it embodies the divine. Fulfil all its needs in a balanced way. Proper amount of exercise — not something serious, but playful will set the tone for the day. And live the whole day as consciously as possible, feeling yourself within your body. Generally we sit, stand, walk and talk and move around as if we are not carrying along our body with ourselves. We mostly drag it. Consciousness each moment will bring an unknown grace and elegance to our body. We just have to decide to be conscious moment to moment and then see the magic happening.

We will find that the body has its own joys. Do anything and really anything — breathing, swimming, jogging — and then sit silently, feeling joy within every fibre of your body. Make every atom of your body alive by giving attention to your body. If you don't feel godly within your body, you won't find God anywhere — be it a temple, *gurudwara*, church, Mecca or Medina. God resides within yourself.

Remember that there is nothing wrong in enjoying physical pleasures. If you don't enjoy your physical pleasure in needful quantity, you become obsessed with it. This obsession will definitely lead to perversions. Then there is a downhill journey which leads to hell. The hell implies disease of your body. All condemnations and denials to our body work as toxins which poison our being and make us unhealthy. Then we are never at ease with our body. This is the real disease.

To be at ease with one's own body is *sahaj yoga*. To be in harmony with one's own body is real health.

Take the first step of meditation: Love your body. Drop all

condemnation and accept your body as the greatest gift of existence. The more you accept it the more healthy and beautiful it becomes. The more you reject it the more you drag yourself and you will become a walking grave. Make your body a temple and not a grave. Live while you are living — full of love and appreciation for your own body. Listen to its needs. Pay total attention and be sincere to it. It will offer you unknown joys and ecstasies. This first step is the right beginning.

Osho reminds us: "The body is the most complex mechanism in existence. It is simply marvellous! Blessed are those who marvel. Begin with the feeling of wonder within your own body, because that is the closest to you. The closest nature has approached you, the closest God has come to you, is through the body. In your body is the water of the oceans, the fire of the stars and the suns, the freshness of the air; and your body is made of earth. Your body represents the whole existence, all the elements. And what a transformation! What a metamorphosis! Look at the earth and then look at your body — what a transformation, and you have never marvelled about it! Dust has become divine; what greater mystery is possible? What greater miracles are you waiting for? And you see the miracle happening every day. Out of the mud arises the lotus...and out of dust has arisen our beautiful body. "

God is in the Gap Between Breaths

God is in the breath inside the breath, said Kabir. He showed that anyone can become illumined from within. Osho once explained a *sutra* from Kabir's song: "Student, tell me what is God?" he asks. He provides the answer: "He is the breath inside the breath."

God is your subjectivity; He is your innerness. Buddha made it a great technique for meditation, watching the breath, because through watching it you will come to know the breath inside the breath. 'Breath' means life. In Sanskrit it is *pran* or life. In Hebrew, the word for breath means spirit. In all languages, breath is synonymous with life, spirit or soul. But breath is not the soul.

Try this experiment: Sitting silently, just watch your breath from the entrance of the nose. When the breath comes in, feel the touch of the breath at the entrance of the nose — watch it there. The touch will be easier to watch; breath will be too subtle. The breath goes in, and you feel it going in: Watch it. And then follow it, go with it. You will find there comes a point where it stops — near your navel, for a tiny moment, for a *pal*. Then it moves outwards again. Follow it — again feel the touch, the breath going out of the nose. Follow it, go with it outside — again you will come to a point when the breath stops for a very tiny moment. Then again the cycle starts.

Inhalation, gap, exhalation, gap, inhalation, gap. That gap is the most mysterious phenomenon inside you. When the breath comes in and stops and there is no movement, that is the point where one can meet God. Or when the breath goes out and stops and there is no movement. Remember, you are not to stop it; it stops on its own. Otherwise, the doer will come in and the witnessing will disappear. You are not to change the breath pattern; you are to neither inhale nor exhale. It is not like *pranayama* of yoga, where you start manipulating the breath. You don't touch the breath at all — you allow its naturalness, its natural flow. When it goes out you follow it; when it comes in you follow it.

Soon you will become aware that there are two gaps. In those two gaps is the door. And in those two gaps you will find that breath itself is not life — maybe a food, not life itself. Because when the breathing stops you are there — you are perfectly conscious. And the breath has stopped, breathing is no more there, and you are there. And once you continue this watching of the breath — what Buddha calls Vipassana or *Anapana-sati* — if you go on watching it, slowly you will see the gap is increasing and becoming bigger. Finally it happens that for minutes together the gap remains. One breath goes in, and then gap... and for minutes the breath does not go out. All has stopped. The world has stopped, time has stopped, thinking has stopped. Because when the breath stops, thinking is not possible. And when the breath stops for minutes together, thinking is absolutely impossible — because the thought process needs continuous oxygen, and your thought process and your breathing are very deeply related.

Your breathing goes on changing with the moods of the mind.

17

God is in the Gap between Breaths

The vice versa is also true — when the breath changes, the moods of the mind change. And when the breath stops, the mind stops. In that stopping of the mind the whole world stops — because the mind is the world. And in that stopping you come to know for the first time what is the breath inside the breath: Life inside life. The liberating experience makes you aware of God — and God is not a person but the experience of life itself.

Awareness

Out of meditation the flowers of virtue arise, bloom. Their fragrance is released to the winds, into the infinity of existence. Buddha gives you only one commandment: awareness. You can call it meditation, you can call it watchfulness. His own word is Sammasati—Right awareness.

—Osho

Awareness is the Criterion

Meditation is a way of life. We cannot separate meditation from life. There are two options in the way we live our life. Either we can live it like a robot mechanically or we can live our lives by being aware, alert and sensitive to every act.

Mystic Kabir says, "*Sadho, jaagat neend na keejey.*"

We don't live, we sleep! Our life is nothing but sleep. We walk in sleep, we talk in sleep and we act in our sleep. Our moments of wakefulness are also shrouded in sleep and darkness. If we look into ourselves we will discover the reason behind this sleep. We have not kindled our lamp of awareness.

Osho says: If you don't take the lamp of awareness with you, you are going to create a hell around you. Light your lamp wherever you go — courting, not courting, is not the point. Wherever you go, whatsoever you do, always do it with the inner light, with awareness. And don't be worried about moralities — about concepts, about what is good and what is bad. Good follows your inner light just like a shadow.

Meditation is taking care of the inner light. It makes us alert. We continue to live the same existence but we are more aware. We make ourselves intense. We eat the same food, walk the same path, live in the same house, stay with our families, but we re-vamp ourselves completely from within. With this meditative awareness you will realise that suddenly the known path is no more the same, because you have evolved. You will notice that the usual food is not the same nor is your family the same because you have evolved.

Everything changes with your inner evolution!

Osho often narrated a beautiful story from the life of Gautama the Buddha. Historically this story might not be true but it has a lot of significance. It conveys a message that helps us learn the truth about life. There are times when fiction is more meaningful than facts.

Gautama Buddha was on his morning walk along with chief disciple Ananda. They were absorbed in a spiritual conversation. A fly came and sat on Buddha's face and his hand made an automatic movement to get rid of the fly. Then suddenly Buddha stopped and made the same movement again. Ananda became puzzled and asked, "*Bhante*, the fly has already left your forehead. Why are you repeating the same movement again?"

Buddha replied, "First time I removed the fly unconsciously. It was done automatically, there was no awareness in my act. Next time I did the same act to remind myself to bring awareness to the act."

Buddha gave us the greatest teaching through this small act. Small actions become great if they are done with awareness. It does not matter if you are doing a great act because if it is done without awareness it becomes meaningless. Awareness is the criterion, and in it lies the true meaning of meditation.

Do Something and get Lost in It

Indians, specially the Hindus all over the world, celebrate the birthday of Lord Krishna, who is worshipped as the total incarnation of God on earth—*purnavtar*. This is not without reason. Neither can it be termed as blind worship or devotion. Krishna deserved it, as he is the only incarnation of God who is multi-dimensional. He was comfortable in all shades and colours of life and he accepted life in totality — whether it was in love and romance or epic war. He faced life in all its extremes — situations of trials and tribulations, tenderness of love and feelings — and celebrated everything. He lived a very colourful life and squeezed all the juice of life that it could offer. He loved life and emerged victorious. Thus he not only had a very significant message — he became the message himself. A message becomes most effective only when it comes out of a real life, the life of the messenger himself. Krishna was the personification of his own message. He is the message for us today.

In his various discourses on Krishna and *Gita*, Osho talks about the relevance of Krishna for the present moment and for the future, emphasising the living of life in totality of the moment and not to be over-concerned with the result. The concern makes our energy divided and we become split. Life demands totality and authenticity.

OSHO FRAGRANCE

Osho reminds us: "In the *Gita*, Krishna says: 'Don't think of the result at all.' It is a message of tremendous beauty and significance and truth. Don't think of the result at all. Just do what you are doing with your totality. Get lost into it. Lose the doer in the doing. Don't be — let your creative energies flow unhindered."

In the divine, a Krishna-like prism, everything is accepted and transformed. But the whole thing is that it is just the same light, and what happens to your life depends on how you respond to this light.

I give you the devil to continuously remind you that millions of people, 99 per cent, waste their lives at first. It is a very poor life; a miserable hell. Everybody has the destiny to reach to the fifth. Krishna has to start dancing in you and then your whole life has to become a celebration. And it is not only that you give back, because when a God gives a gift to you, it doesn't look good to give the same gift back. It has to be transformed. If it comes as one light, it has to go as seven. If it comes as one single note, you have to return a whole orchestra.

Living life in all the dimensions authentically, playfully is the core message of Krishna's life. It is *raas*, an unending *raas* and his *Leela*. Osho says: "Leeladhar is one of the names of Krishna. He is the most playful God, the most non-serious; there is no comparison to him. He was totally into life, into all dimensions of life, and he enjoyed everything — from love to war, everything; there is no denial in him. He can be good, he can be bad; he can be truthful, he can be deceitful. He can sacrifice himself, he can cheat you. He is very spontaneous, without any ideals and without any ideology... just a man living from moment to moment, responding, not with any *a priori* idea. He has no idea of how

23

things should be. He functions out of his totality, and whatsoever happens out of that totality is good. He has no definition of goodness other than that."

Come, Come, whoever You are...

I have heard, that in times of crisis, human consciousness takes a leap and evolves to a higher level to meet the challenge.

But in today's world, with conflicts and troubles raging all around, one is prone to conclude that depressive atheistic existentialists seem to have wrong notions of man's nature. They call themselves existentialists but don't think of man in his entirety, the totality of body, mind and soul. They believe that a man is only a mind and nothing else. The man in reality is much more than just a mind! A man's existence consists of the physical dimension of body, a deeper dimension of the emotions and feelings of heart while the third dimension is of thought, which is the most superfluous dimension; rather a luxury item. The final dimension is the transcendental, the dimension of being; call it soul or spirit. I don't think that the existentialist philosophers of the superfluous dimension can deal effectively with the raw zealots who are ruled by their beastly impulsiveness. They should think again before they launch into this ridiculous adventure.

And these existentialist therapists plan, "There they will drink coffee and talk animatedly about the absurd nature of life and man's lonely isolation in the universe. They will be accompanied by a number of heartbreakingly beautiful young men on mopeds in Versace striped T-shirts and who will propagate fear, uncertainty and doubt by looking remote and unattainable."

This remedy is nothing new or original. It is the same as the misguided priests of almost all the religions have tried on men. The indoctrination of fear and greed has not worked — rather it has led to more violence in the world. The policy of fear has poisoned man since eternity. Man belongs to existence. This existence is his home. By propagating fear and creating a feeling of isolation in human heart, you are giving him a cancerous outlook, which is the root cause of hatred and violence.

Teach them human values of love and reverence for life, as all life on earth is sacred. Teach them of existence that dwells in all of us. Killing others is equal to killing oneself as life is just another name of God. Life itself is God.

The whole of humanity is suffering from war fatigue. It needs to be rejuvenated with love and songs and dance of life. Let the Rubaiyat of Omar Khayyam play and so let the *dervish* dances of Mevlana Jelaluddin Rumi and other Sufi masters bring ecstasy to the people of war-torn regions if the world. Osho gives us message of the Mevlana who says:

Come, Come, whoever you are;

Wanderer, worshipper, lover of learning... It does not matter.

Ours is not a caravan of despair.

Come, even if you have broken your vow a thousand times.

Come, come, yet again come.

Come, come, whoever you are...sinner, unconscious, living a life which is not glorious, divine, meaningful; living a life which has no poetry, no joy, a life of hell.... whosoever you are, Mevlana says, "Come, I am ready to receive you. Be my guest!"

Dreaming and the Inner Self

Enlightened mystic Chuang Tzu was one of the greatest Taoist masters in China. He was also famous for the art of story-telling. Once he dreamt that he had become a butterfly, fluttering here and there. In the dream he had no awareness of his individuality as a person. He was only a butterfly. Suddenly, he awoke and found himself lying there as a person. But then he thought to himself, 'Was I before a man who dreamt about being a butterfly, or am I now a butterfly who dreams about being a man?'

He called all his disciples and asked this question. The disciples were confused and could not answer. He told them to meditate over this and come back on discovering the answer. Nobody came back with any answer and the question remains unanswered to this day.

Dreams have their own mystery and sometimes it becomes very difficult to decipher their meaning. Experts both in the East and the West have been trying to analyse them and trying to create a science of dreams.

John Sanford, a Jungian analyst, writes in his book, *Dreams and Healing*: "The unconscious is the great source of our energy.

Meditation upon dreams helps us tap into it. Remembering dreams is like irrigating a field, watering a garden, or planting seeds in the ground."

A lot of study has been going on in the West about dreams. The West has created a huge analytical science around dreaming; dreams are analysed to study human problems and maladies. Though I don't consider this as a totally futile exercise, because lots of startling discoveries have emerged through this process, yet it is not absolute to understanding human situations.

Indian yoga also talks about the three states of *jagrit, sushupti,* and *swapna* (waking, sleeping and dreaming) and the fourth that is beyond and is called *turiya*. The *yogic* process is whether one is in *jagrit, sushupti* or *swapna* state, one has not to give too much importance to these states; rather one has to remember the fourth, the *turiya* — the transcendental — the witnessing consciousness. *Turiya* is the real health: "Don't analyse your dreams, your sleep, your wakefulness. Watch the one that goes through all these states. Sure there must be something that goes through all these states. Settle in that state."

Sanskrit and Hindi language have a beautiful word for health: *Swasthya*. It means *swa*, the self; and *thya* means settled. Being settled in one's own being, the inner self is the real health. You are *swastha* when you are settled in your inner self. So there is nothing to analyse; these things are not worth analysing. These states have to be transcended to realise your inner self. The real health is experienced in transcendence.

Western psychology asks: "What undiscovered possibilities are present in your dreams? What suggestion does your inner self have for your waking life?" And it answers: "Our dreams offer us many other ways of being in the world, perhaps more assertive, compassionate, creative, discerning. It is the attention we give to our inner being — whether through dreams, meditation or other spiritual practices — that we expand our capacity for greater energy and creativity in our waking lives."

This is an utterly confused approach — mixing dreaming with meditation. Meditation has nothing to do with dreaming. Meditation even goes beyond our ordinary wakefulness, leave alone dreaming. Zen considers it as absolute nonsense.

There's a story of a Zen Master who woke up one morning. Sitting in his bed, he called out to one of his disciples and said, "Last night I saw a dream; can you analyse this dream for me?" The disciple went out and came back with a jug of water and told the Master, "Here, please wash your face." And went away.

The Master called out to another disciple and told him the same. The other disciple also went out and came back with a cup of tea. Then the master called to his chief disciple and told him about the dream. The disciple said: "Yes, I do have the answer to your problem." Saying this he went out and returned with a big bucket of water and poured the whole bucket on him and told him: "Master, please wake up now. Enough is enough."

Now, this is the true Eastern approach to our dreams. If any of his disciples had started analysing the dream, the Master would have thrown him out of the monastery. This would have been a disqualification for the disciple.

And the whole effort in the East has been totally different. We have never bothered about the meaning of dreams. Our whole effort is to make others aware so that dreams disappear.

Osho says this is the right interpretation: "You had a dream? Wash your face, be finished! Still lingering a little? Have a cup of tea, but get out of it! It is a dream! What is there to interpret?"

Only one thing has to be remembered: You dreamed because you were unconscious. And now you are trying to interpret it; still you are clinging to it. It happened because you were fast asleep.

For a Buddha dreams disappear; they don't happen, they cannot happen, because he becomes so alert that even in sleep a subtle layer of awareness remains. He never loses his awareness. That's what Krishna means when he says in the *Gita*, "When everybody is fast asleep, the *yogi* is awake."

Mother India, Brother Indian

The actual truth is that India cannot be explained by philosophy only, as India does not believe in philosophy — it never did. The Indian heart throbs with mysticism. This is the principal reason that for thousands of years India has been producing first-class mystics and second-rate philosophers. There's a whole lineage of mystics who have delved deep into the mysteries of life and discovered a treasure of diamonds from the depths of unfathomable oceans. They stand out as the shining stars high in the sky. India calls them the enlightened ones, not philosophers.

Ashtavakra, Buddha, Mahavira, Patanjali, Shankara, Kabir, Nanak, Bodhidharma, Gorakh—they were all mystics and *rishis*. The Sanskrit word *rishi* simply means 'the enlightened poet'. And these sages are the ones who have influenced India down the ages, shaped the Indian way of life and carved the collective consciousness of this country. Every Indian carries something of that collective consciousness in him, with him. It's not intellectually understandable; it cannot be understood by the cerebrum simply because it is not mathematical. It cannot be derived through formulae of logic; it is mystical.

Philosophy depends on mathematics. It's a very scientific

attitude that has been religiously followed by the West. That is why it gave birth to first-rate scientists and philosophers and could create certain systems of philosophy. The whole progress of the West owes all this to its logical and systematic approach of the mind. The West has made an incredible achievement as far as the outside world of materialism is concerned. India envies it but cannot compete with it. It will always lag behind.

When we try to do something that's not natural to our being, we cannot reach too far. We are left far behind in the race. We start finding excuses or start to ridicule the achievements of the West, but we won't accept what is natural to them and us: We are more at ease with the mystical approach and they are more comfortable with the philosophical approach. Both approaches are unique and complimentary to each other, like day and night, man and woman and so on so forth.

We compete with each other because we do not understand each other. When we understand each other, we stop competing and become complementary to each other. This complementariness is inter-dependence. We need materialism as much as we need mysticism. The mysticism does not give us food and shelter while materialism does not fulfill our inner vacuum. The void within keeps expanding. We become utterly hollow and the Western philosophy or science does not help to fill that void. In the West, material richness has not reduced the suicide rate; rather it has increased it. The reason is hopelessness. In India poverty may be one of the main reasons of suicides, though both the situations have their respective exceptions.

Coming back to the original question, "What is Indian?" perhaps the answer is that it is something irrational, something illogical, something mystical. What is more illogical than being

MOTHER INDIA, BROTHER INDIAN

blissful in utter poverty? A Buddha becomes a beggar and attains to ultimate blissfulness while we encounter so many beggars on traffic lights in India and they really look a miserable lot. We touch the feet of the Buddha while we avoid these beggars like pests. We can be certain that both the Buddha and the beggars represent India.

On the contrary who represents the West? Alexander the Great and Einstein represent the West. One tried to conquer the world; the other created the atom bomb to threaten the existence of the world. In India, we have known and worshipped different kinds of conquerors like Mahavir, the Jina who conquered themselves — conquered their inner enemies like greed, anger, lust — and they teach the same to the whole world. So, when the Western mind sends an Alexander to conquer India, he conquers nothing; he returns empty-handed. Indians have allowed all the conquerors to come to India and plunder the country for the people could not resist them; but this submission has been significant. Many Alexanders got absorbed by India in this process and were conquered, instead of winning over India.

Ultimately nobody has been able to conquer India, because India functions on a different plane. It is like a spiritual mother to the whole world. Mother welcomes you to nourish you. How can you conquer your mother? Ultimately it's her love that wins. For this reason precisely we call our country: Mother India.

India is mother to all and an Indian is a brother to all.

Rising in Love

L ife does not exist in isolation. It exists in inter-dependent relationships. Our relationships exist on many levels of consciousness. We may not be aware that we are not only related to our near and dear ones but to whatever exists on this planet or in universe. We are related to the earth, the air, the sky and the sun, the trees, birds and the animals — all forms of nature. Theirs is an organic unity and connectivity of life in all forms. But what matters to us most is our human relationships — between the lover and the beloved, the wife and the husband, the mother and the children, sisters and brothers. These relationships are distinguishable because of certain degrees of attachment that we come to experience in such relationships.

We are related to the earth, the sun and moon, the air, the water, the fire and all elements of nature. Actually we cannot live without them for a single day. Though we are totally dependent on the natural elements and have a close relationship like that of the mother and children, it is surprising that we do not feel any attachment with them as we feel in our blood relationships or even with friends. We know that the relationship between the five elements and us are also part of our blood. They rule our emotions and thoughts, hearts and minds, but it is in our human relationships that we become emotionally involved with and the element of attachment creeps in. We become so entangled and involved that we feel that at a certain point we come to realise that we cannot live without them. Life seems to be unbearable without them.

Love in all our relationships in its first stage manifests as an attachment. A child becomes possessive of the mother and father, and the same attachment and possessiveness is there between the child and playthings — the toys and dolls. And then the child grows up and becomes young and starts falling in love with the opposite sex and the attachment takes a different form. The young person becomes attached to the lover or the beloved and becomes possessive, finds it difficult to live without these relationships. This attachment may go to the level of the question of life and death. We see some people committing suicides when frustrated of failure in relationships or even killing others in desperation. This attachment shows the intensity of crudeness of love. And there's this reason for which we say that the person has "fallen in love". This certainly is a fall. Today, love exists on such a low level that it becomes an abysmal ditch.

This attachment is not healthy love and does not nourish people. It is a stagnant kind of love and lacks the evolution in consciousness. Love stops falling into the ditch and starts rising only when we grow in consciousness. The element of meditation and consciousness in love makes it refined and sensitivity gives wings to it and helps it to move upward. Then people grow in love. The falling in love becomes rising in love. Love becomes capable of sharing without demanding anything in return. Love knows the joy of giving without any expectation of getting anything in return. Love becomes unconditional and helps the other person rise to the same level.

Osho Fragrance

Falling in love leads to misery invariably while rising in love leads to bliss in relationships. This love functions with trust and not with fear or sense of insecurity. Real love knows no insecurity or fear. This love functions in freedom and not possessiveness, as it trusts totally and knows how to let go.

Attachment is very gravitational and earthly but freedom in love gives wings to it so that it becomes capable of flying high in the sky. True love needs to be rooted in the earth and also needs wings to fly in the sky. It needs nourishment from both the earth and the sky. Love is a multi-coloured rainbow between the earth and the sky. Osho said: "Love is both. It is rich and it is painful, it is agony and it is ecstasy — because love is the meeting of the earth and the sky, of the known and the unknown, of the visible and the invisible. Love is the boundary that divides matter and consciousness, the boundary of the lower and the higher. Love has roots in the earth; that is, its pain, its agony. And love has its branches in the sky; that is its ecstasy. Love is not a single phenomenon; it is dual. It is a rope stretched between two polarities."

Falling in love leads also to lust and in becoming unconscious in lust kills love. Osho said: "Lust is greed, lust is attachment, lust is possessiveness. Love needs no possession, love knows no attachment, because love is not greed. Love is a gift. It is a sharing. You have found something; your heart is full, your fruits are ripe. You hanker that somebody should come and share. It is unconditional; who shares does not matter. But you are so full of it that you would like to be unburdened — as when clouds are full of rain-water, they rain.

"Sometimes they rain in a forest, sometimes they rain on a hill, sometimes they rain in a desert, but they rain. The fact of where they rain is irrelevant. They are so full they have to rain. A lover is so full he becomes a cloud, full of love-water; he has to rain. That raining is spontaneous."

Life Exists in Polar Opposites

Life exists in polar opposites – darkness and light, day and night, good and bad and divine and devil. There also are the polarities of masculine and feminine, like the negative and positive poles of electricity, or energy — Tao in China describes it as *yin* and *yang*. All these polarities are inseparable and constitute an organic whole. We worship the divine and despise the devil. We want only one pole of existence — only goody-goody, nothing baddy-baddy. And it is not possible; it is simply impossible. Because that is not the way existence functions! It works only through polar opposites. Because the tension between these two poles is not just that but is also complimentary to the existence of each other.

For every Rama there's a Ravana. For every Krishna there's a Kansa. For every Mahatma Gandhi there's a Godse. Apparently there is the interplay of two opposite existences, but essentially they are one whole — the organic whole. Once this becomes clear to us, we are at ease with the whole drama that this life unfolds before us. Though I know it is not very easy to accept both facets simultaneously. It is certainly very difficult to accept life in its totality, when we have always accepted the sugary-sweet and discarded the bitter and keep on doing the same. We want sweet dreams and no nightmares. We want only saints and no sinners in the world. Do you think it is possible? Only saints! Then it will not be the same world — at least not this world that we know. It will be a paradise or something else. The world has to have saints and sinners together. Saints will go out of business without the sinners. Same fate will be in store for the police, the judges and all will go out of business without criminals. Their existence is interdependent. Life is basically an interdependence of polar opposites. Here the saint's survival depends on the existence of the sinners. *Sannyasis* depend on *sansaris*.

Once Osho wrote a letter to one of his disciples and said that he saw both the aspects within himself. He wrote: "I am one with all things — in beauty, in ugliness, for whatsoever it is — there I am. Not only in virtue but in sin too I am a partner, and not only heaven but hell too is mine. Buddha, Jesus, Lao Tzu — it is easy to be their heir, but Genghis, Timur and Hitler? They are also within me! No, not half — I am the whole of mankind! Whatsoever is man's is mine — flowers and thorns, darkness as well as light, and if nectar is mine, whose is poison? Nectar and poison — both are mine. Whoever experiences this I call religious, for only the anguish of such experience can revolutionise life on earth."

Get rid of Ego and Attain Bliss

G. K. Chesterton, one of the most profound thinkers of the world, has said, "The angels fly because they take themselves lightly." Taking oneself lightly or taking everything lightly is really a religious quality which is rarely found even in the so-called religious people. Religious people, who are supposed to be humble and soft, often consider themselves special and holier than others. They develop a certain ego. Ordinary people who run after money, power and prestige have an ordinary ego, which is visible. Religious people have a pious ego.

A person full of ego — ordinary or pious — becomes too self-conscious and serious. Such a person cannot understand life as *leela*, the inter-play of existence, the creativity of God. For that one needs the lightness of ego-lessness. For that one needs to experience an inner light in one's being. This realisation happens with the disappearance or evaporation of ego and one experiences oneness with the universe.

Osho said: "That has been the ultimate goal of the mystics — to disappear into the universe, not to be separate; to melt and merge into the universe. Separation brings anxiety, death and misery. We are miserable because we feel separate from God or the universe. Blis arises whenever you feel one with the universe; when you are in harmony with the universe, bliss arises. There is great joy, rejoicing; you disappear, you die in a way, but you are reborn. You are reborn as the ocean, you die as the dewdrop."

Buddha said: "Existence is one. There are no boundaries. Nobody is separate from anybody else. We live in one ocean of consciousness. We are one consciousness — deluded by the boundaries of the body, deluded by the boundaries of the mind."

And because of the body and the mind, and because of the identification with the body and mind, we think we are separate, we think we are selves. This is how we create the ego.

Osho elaborated: "When I say drop the ego, I mean drop all demarcation lines. You are not separate from life, you are part of it. Like a wave, you are part of the ocean. You are not separate at all. Neither as a saint are you separate, nor as a sinner are you separate. You are not separate at all. You are one with life. You are neither dependent on life, nor are you independent of life — you are interdependent. When you understand that we are all interdependent, linked with each other, life becomes one; we are just manifestations of it... then you start becoming blissful."

The Body is a Temple for the Soul

Soul is immortal. Or should one say that what is immortal is the soul. The body is the embodiment of our soul. The soul can exist — and it does exist — without the body, but the body cannot exist without the soul.

The soul is immortal. The body is important for the realisation that one is not just a body, rather one is the soul. This realisation also depends on being in the body. In fact, the body is the temple for the soul.

In a particular sect, people fast for a long time — so long as the soul does not leave the body. It is their conscious effort to make the soul free from the embodiment. And this makes the *muni* respectable, because he starves his body so much that his soul finds it impossible to continue in the body.

This is allowed by the philosophy of a particular sect though it is inconceivable to the believers of the other religions. The law of the country also does not allow any kind of suicide, but law does not interfere with this process of leaving the body by a *muni*. In ancient times, the sages spent their last days in the coldest regions of the Himalayas, fasting and practising a particular meditative *anushthan* which helped to shed their body and let their soul become one with the universe.

Committing suicide out of frustration or depression is not the same. It does not make you feel elevated or liberated. The soul has to be reborn and seek the body again for the attainment of self-realisation.

Spiritual journey is death and rebirth on a very different level. It is the death of our ego. In the *Sacred Yes*, Osho said: "Something will be born out of that death, something immensely superior. But that birth is possible only if death happens first. Initiation means death in the deep trust that resurrection will happen. Initiation means crucifixion in the faith that resurrection will follow. Hence the orange colour has been chosen for *sannyas*: it is the colour of fire.

"The ego has to be burned to ashes. *Sannyas* is really what the symbol of Phoenix in the West represents. When Phoenix is burnt in the fire, nothing is left; then a totally new life arises. Each death is a beginning; the greater the death, the greater will be the beginning. If the death is total, then total will be the beginning. We have to pay by dying; that courage is needed. To be a *sannyasin* is the greatest courage possible, because there is no greater adventure in life; all else is trivial and mundane."

Be Aware and Live Intensely

The enlightened mystics teach us to live our life with full intensity. But most of us conduct our lives as if in a daze. Real awakening needs certain intensity. Lack of intensity creates boredom. It is only when we are face to face with a dangerous situation that we become fully awake and fully conscious.

Osho once told the story of a Sufi mystic, Bayazid, who used to talk to his disciples about awareness, and they would ask, "What is awareness? You keep on talking about it."

One day he took them to the river. On both sides there was a small hill. He said, "We are going to put a long wooden bridge — just one foot wide — from this end to the other, and you have to walk on it. And then you will know what awareness is."

They replied, "But we have been walking our whole life, and we have never come to know."

He said, "Wait," and he did the experiment.

Many of them, who became scared, said: "We cannot walk. Just one foot wide?"

"But how much do you need to walk on? When you are walking on the earth, you can walk on a one-foot-wide strip easily. Why can't you walk on a one-foot-wide strip hanging between two hills?" he asked his disciples.

A few people tried. They took a few steps but then came back, and said, "It is dangerous." Then Bayazid walked and a few followed him. When they reached the other side, those who followed him fell at his feet and said, "Master, now we know what awareness is. The danger was so much that we could not afford to walk in slumber. We had to be alert. Any wrong step and we would have gone forever."

Osho said: "Awareness means an intensity. Such an intensity of wakefulness that no thought interferes. You are simply conscious without any thought. Try it. You can try it anywhere. While walking on a road, every moment is danger. Here, every moment is risky as it can turn into death. You are all crossing the plank with a mountainous burden on you; just a small slip and you are gone. You have to be alert, so alert that no other energy is left in you; everything has become just a flame of awareness."

46

Usher in the Age of Enlightenment

The world has progressed much beyond our imagination. But this progress has been on the outside. Not much has changed in the inner world of man who continues to remain almost the same. The same anger, lust, politics and violence remain, only expressions have changed. Now the time has come that we transform the inner world of man to create a balance between the outer and the inner. We must plant the seeds of meditation on a vast scale and nourish the seeds, so that they flower everywhere.

47

This flowering will usher in the age of enlightenment as never witnessed before.

Yes, we did witness this age of enlightenment in the times of Buddha and Mahavira, but that was only in India. Now this is possible in the entire world.

Osho has said: "The world can come to a harmony if meditation is spread far and wide, and people are brought to one consciousness within themselves... Only when there are many people who are pools of peace, silence, understanding, will war disappear. It is only a question of understanding the value of meditation. Then it is possible for millions to become undivided within themselves. They will be the first humans to become harmonious. And their harmoniousness, their beauty, their compassion, their love — all their qualities — are bound to resound around the world."

Science has transformed the outer world. The inner world too can be transformed with the science of spirituality.

Feeling Functions

L ife is a process of learning. We stop growing when we stop learning. What we learn from outside sources is tuition. And there's another source within us, that of intuition. The two are distinct dimensions of learning — one from outside to inside and vice versa.

Between tuition and intuition is the difference of 'in'. This is the dimension of meditation. In Hindi, we talk of *antardrishti*, translated as 'inner eye' or 'insight'. This belongs to the dimension of intuition.

49

Osho explains this beautifully in the following words. He said: "Intellect lives on tuition. Others have to teach you. Intuition comes from within; it grows out of you and is a flowering of being. This is the quality of consciousness without a centre. Timelessness; or you can call it the now, the present. But remember, it is not present between past and future; it is the present in which past and future have dissolved."

Talking of intuition, Osho says: "The word is significant. We are given tuition everywhere. That is to repress intuition. In schools, colleges, universities, you are given tuition. It means something from outside being forced on you, and intuition means something from your core. If unconscious, it will remain instinct.

"If you are conscious, instinct plus awareness equal intuition. Then for the first time you have found your Master within you. Intuition is your Master, your real university. And now you don't need a scripture, you don't need any guide. Your inner light is enough to lead you to the ultimate goal of enlightenment."

Normally, a human being functions on three levels — instinct, intellect and intuition. Instinct is of the physical level. Animals possess it. Intellect is functioning of the head; one needs to be human to have intellect. Intuition is deeper; one needs to have his heart functioning properly. Behind these is our being, whose only quality is witnessing.

Osho says: "The head only thinks; hence it never comes to a conclusion. It is verbal, linguistic, logical but because it has no roots in reality, thousands of years of philosophical thinking have not given us a single conclusion. Philosophy has been the greatest exercise in futility.

"Beyond intellect is feeling. Another name for this is intuition, a more scientific name. But few reach intuition, because for that you have to go beyond intellect. Meditation is the only way. Unfortunately, meditation is not part of our education. It stops at intellect, creating a quarrel between instinct and intellect, creating a schizophrenia."

If you meditate, something beyond intellect starts functioning. You can call it the heart, intuition. It has no arguments but tremendous experiences. But it is not the end of your nature. Like instinct, on the other polarity of your being, beyond the mind — which is the world of intellect — is a world of intuition.

"This opens doors through meditation, which is simply knocking on doors of intuition; intuition is also completely ready; it does not grow; you have inherited that from existence."

That's what meditation is about: 'Dropping the mind and moving to the heart.' A leap from thinking to feeling, intellect to intuition. Head to heart.

Determination Opens Many Doors

We often say we are seeking truth or searching for God and we want our life to be peaceful, contented and blissful. We make efforts to attain all this but our efforts don't produce any results. We become more frustrated than before. This is all because our efforts are lukewarm and our quest has no real determination and strength.

Osho once told the story of a Sufi saint, Farid. A man once asked him the way to attain God, Farid looked into his eyes and saw thirst. He was on his way to the river, so he asked the man to accompany him and promised to show him the way to attain God after they'd bathed.

They arrived at the river and as soon as the man plunged, Farid grabbed the man's head and pushed it down into the water with great force. The man began to struggle to free himself from Farid's grip.

He was much weaker than the saint but his latent strength gradually began to stir and soon it became impossible for the saint to hold him down. The man pushed himself to the limit and was eventually able to get out of the river. He was shocked. Farid was laughing loudly.

After the man calmed down, the saint asked him, "When you were under the water what desires did you have in your mind?"

He replied, "Desires! There weren't desires; there was just one desire — to get a breath of air."

The saint replied, "This is the secret of attaining God. This is determination. And your determination awakened all your latent powers."

In a real moment of intense determination, great strength is generated — and a man can pass from the world into truth; by determination one can awaken from the dream to the truth.

A Mature Mind is a Religious Mind

Life is an ocean of one consciousness. As individuals we appear to be all separate, just like waves of an ocean. But essentially we are all one, as an ocean is. We are dreaming when we claim to have our private or individual existence. It is a dream because it is an appearance; it is not an existential reality.

Do you know how one wave is separate from another wave? Yes, the waves may dream or think that they are separate. But ask the ocean: Are they separate? Ocean knows no separation. Ocean does not know that there are waves, because it is the ocean itself that is waving. It knows itself as an organic unity.

In this state of appearance or *maya*, as the wise sages describe, the waves think they are separate and this leads to conflicts and quarrels between the waves. Then some sage amongst these declares: "Come on you guys! You are not really separate. Why are you fighting?"

The waves are busy beings as Hindus and Muslims and Christians and have become very hardened and solid in such fictitious identities. The waves are struggling hard to defend and protect their imagined identities. They have their claims of superiority and holier-than-thou attitude. And they tend to forget their real holiness: A holy person is one who feels one with the whole, one with the ocean of consciousness, the cosmic consciousness, the Brahman! What *Upanishads* declare: *Aham Brahmasmi.*

Osho explained: "To be whole is to be holy. There is no other way to be holy; just be whole. Divisions within you must fall; you must become a unity. But you are a conflict. You have become many, you are not one; you are a crowd. Neurosis comes out of it; madness comes out of it."

"It is said that when Moses went to the hill to meet his God, the bush was afire and from behind the bush he heard, 'Stop! Take your shoes off. This is holy ground'. I have always liked it, loved it. But all ground is holy ground and all bushes are afire with God. If you have not seen this yet, you have missed much.

"Look again. All bushes are afire with God and from every bush comes the commandment, 'Stop and take your shoes off. It is holy ground you are walking on.' All ground, the whole earth, the whole existence is sacred. Once you have that feeling entering you, I will call you mature — not before that.

"A mature mind is a religious mind."

The *Vedas* hold the Source of Knowledge

When the sages during the Vedic ages wrote the *Upanishads*, they were trying to share their wisdom with the generations to come. They did not even bother to have their names given to the *Upanishads* because the wisdom and knowledge did not belong to them — they were merely the mediums of the divine or godliness. They had experienced oneness with the ultimate, the consciousness. Osho defines the *Veda* as the authentic knowledge about the inner one.

The *Veda* is the supreme science: Science of the inner one, science of subjectivity, science of the knower, not of the known, science of the consciousness itself. Now, we hear from Germany that they have patented even the name *Veda*. It's sad that everything in the West is turned into a commercial venture, even the inner experience of enlightenment. Consciousness is not a commodity or an object to be copyrighted or trademarked.

The *Veda* is essentially the realm of consciousness and inner growth process that is painful. Osho defined this phenomenon: "Consciousness makes you human. And this is the beauty of it; that whenever you are conscious, suffering disappears. Suffering brings in consciousness, but if you move more and more in consciousness, suffering disappears."

In Sanskrit, there is a beautiful word for suffering. It is called *vedana*, and *vedana* has two meanings: One suffering; the other, knowledge. *Vedana* comes from the same root as *Veda*. *Veda* means the source of knowledge. Those who coined the word, *vedana*, came to know a fact, that suffering is knowledge. Hence, they used the same root word for both.

If you suffer, immediately you become aware; it comes into your consciousness. That's why medical science, particularly Ayurveda, defines health as bodilessness; if you don't know the body you are healthy; if you know the body, something is wrong because knowing exists only when something goes wrong. If you become really aware, you don't become involved in the wrong.

On the contrary, you grow in your awareness. Also once you are aware you come to know that there is disease, discomfort and suffering around you. Once you are aware, all bridges are broken and the gap is immediately present there. You can see: The body suffers, but the identification is broken. Suffering brings in awareness, awareness breaks the identification — and that is the key to life.

Prayer Cleans Your Soul

In the book of Mirdad, the author Mikhail Naimy said: "You need no lip or tongue for praying. But you need a silent heart, a master wish, a master thought and above all, a master will that neither doubts nor hesitates. For words are of no avail except that the heart be present and awake in every syllable. And when the heart is present and awake, the tongue had better go to sleep, or hide behind sealed lips."

The mystic Mirdad revealed the real mystery of prayer which is the fragrance of heart that has been purified by the cleansing process of meditation. Without deep meditation, our prayer becomes the by-product of our conditioning. Then it is merely the prayer of Hindu or Muslim conditioning. The real prayer is beyond all this conditioning. For such a prayer to happen, the temples made of bricks or human hands may not be very helpful. It may naturally happen in the natural, uncorrupted environs of vast oceans and high mountains, lush green wilderness, where the human heart naturally bows down in awe. Prayer is that feeling where the human heart feels surrounded by godliness.

Osho explains this phenomenon: "Prayer can happen anywhere. You need not go to the temple to pray, but wherever you pray, you create a temple, an invisible temple. Wherever somebody bows down in prayer to existence, that place becomes sacred.

"To a praying heart, any stone becomes *kaaba*, any water becomes Ganges water. To a praying heart, each tree is a Bodhi tree. The question is not of formality; it is of the feeling of being, uplifted. Yes, exactly that's what prayer is: When you suddenly feel you are being uplifted, when gravitation has no more pull over you, when you know that all the weight has disappeared, that you are weightless; when there is no past hanging around your neck like a rock, and when there is no future distracting you, driving you away from the present — when THIS moment is all, THIS HERE, THIS MOMENT, is all in all, something opens up in the heart and a fragrance is released. Sometimes in words, sometimes in silence. Sometimes in meaningful words, and sometimes just like a child babbling. Sometimes it may become a song, or a dance. Sometimes you may just be sitting like a Buddha — utterly quiet, unmoving."

There is nothing official about prayer. There exists no law about prayer. It is a love affair between a human heart and the existence or life. Life is the unofficial temple of prayer. Mirdad was right when he said: "Nor have you any needs of temples to pray in. Whoever cannot find a temple in his heart, can never find his heart in any temple."

The Real Conquest

Meditating on a deeper level, I feel that cruel people die only physically; in reality they never really die. They continue living forever, as on a positive side, people like Gautam Buddha and Mahavira continue living in the hearts and minds of people. Their physical death never brings an end to their influence on the beings of people. They are such a powerful force, all the Buddhas and Mahaviras and the Hitlers and the likes of him in this world.

The negative forces are as strong as positive forces. Buddhas are all the enlightened sages who influence seekers of truth and become a force of transformation in the lives of seekers who further share their peace and creativity with the world. Hitler influenced those who were not interested in their own transformation but interested in dominating others. These are the two clear-cut categories and there are other shades in between also. But what is absolutely clear is that as the godly incarnations keep appearing in the world, the incarnations of Hitler also make their regular appearances in the world. Osho talked about the influence of murderers like Genghis Khan or Tamerlane or Adolf Hitler on people. He said: "The ghost of Adolf Hitler, his long shadow, is still present. And Adolf Hitler is not something that you can confine to one person. It is something deep down in the German mind itself. Adolf Hitler would not have existed if the German mind had not been supportive of him."

And not only ordinary people — who can be easily influenced, impressed — but many exceptional people: Geniuses like Heidegger, who is certainly the most important philosopher of the 20th century. He was a follower of Adolf Hitler. What these people saw in Adolf Hitler was something that was in themselves. In Hitler it was magnified. In themselves they could not see it, but Hitler became the mirror; they could see it, and he became the representative of the collective unconscious mind of Germany. Hence, the influence that he had. And Germany has suffered through Adolf Hitler's influence so much, that the wound is still there and it hurts.

We are living in a wounded world and the wounds have gone deep into the human psyche. The wounded people avoid transforming themselves and are desperate to conquer the world. Mahavira, the twenty-fourth *Tirthankara* was also a great conqueror who taught the seekers of the world to conquer themselves. This is the real conquest and it happens without any violence to anybody.

Sensitivity Helps to Discover *Dharma*

What is *dharma*? Down the centuries this question has always been discussed and debated by philosophers, thinkers, religionists and even scientists and they all have differed with each other. But there are other mystics who have been in complete agreement with each other about this. Saint Dadu said: "*Sabai sayane ek mat.*"

A seeker once asked the Buddhist Master, Bodhidharma: "What is *dharma*?"

He replied: "It was never produced, and will never be reduced; therefore it is called *dharma*, the norm of the universe."

Osho defined *dharma* as the ultimate law, the law of all the laws. "*Dharma* is a special Sanskrit word. It means exactly what in Chinese is meant by *Tao* or what in Greek stands for *logos*. In all these three languages, it means the same — the ultimate law. It is not any particular law — like the laws of science. These scientific laws are merely limited manifestations or expressions of the one universal law — the one that holds all such laws in itself is called *dharma*. *Dharma is* the inherent nature of everything that exists — or the existence itself.

"Being one with existence, feeling oneness with all that

exists is the real religiousness and is much above being just a Hindu, Muslim, Buddhist or Christian. These are also the limited expressions or manifestations of the universal law, the ultimate law that is *dharma*. *Dharma* is the wholeness, interwoven-ness, inter-relatedness, inner connectivity of all that which exists beyond the limits of our understanding or perception. This may be understood logically or intellectually, but to understand it in reality, one has to dissolve into it and feel oneness with it."

Osho said: "Through intellect you can discover particular laws. Only through sensitivity can you discover the universal law. The universal is not available to the intellect. That's the difference between science and religion."

And he added: "So, start feeling for the universe. Just sitting silently, listen to the universe. Remember more and more to be non-intellectual and sensitive, and then you will know that there is a universal law. And to know the universal law is to know all — nothing else is needed. Then by knowing it, one by and by dissolves into it. By knowing it, one is overpowered by it. And when your life is run by the universal law and you are no more a doer, then you have a true life — the life of benediction and bliss."

63

Just *Jalebis*

The other day a Western guest who had the opportunity of relishing a piece of *jalebi* (a sweetmeat), expressed his amazement about its shape and sweetness, inquiring how it was made. My friend tried to explain the method, describing it in Indian English: "Round and round and round... full stop."

Yes, the *jalebi* is a peculiar sweet in that it represents the philosophy of life and death. A *jalebi's* circles are circles of life. It's full stop means the point of death. We move endlessly in circles, then comes death. The end that is not real because we are born again and restart the same game. Enlightened people like the Buddha called it a vicious circle, a wheel which moves on. We are like spokes of the wheel. Sometimes we come up, sometimes we go down.

The wheel goes on moving, up and down, life and death. One moment of success, another of failure; one of hope, another of despair. It has been going on for eternity.

Explaining Eastern wisdom in practical terms, Osho says, "You love a woman, your mind hankers for repetition. Why? Why hanker for the same experience? You eat food, you hanker for it again. Why?"

The reason is whatever you do, you never do it totally. Something remains discontented. If you do it totally, there will be no hankering for repetition and you will be searching for the new, exploring the unknown.

You will not move in a vicious circle; your life will become growth. Ordinarily people move in circles. They appear to move but they only seem to. He further adds, "There is a great and urgent need to do something one has never done before — a search for yourself. You have run after everything in the world and it has not led anywhere. All roads go round and round; never reaching a goal. They don't have a goal."

Visualising this perspective, one suddenly becomes sick of action, anger, fights, love affairs, greed and jealousy. This is the foundation of Eastern wisdom. It creates great boredom with life, death and the vicious circle.

That is the original meaning of samsara. It means the wheel that goes on moving without a stop. An awakened person jumps out of this vicious circle and starts living each moment in full awareness.

Spiritual growth means we stop moving in circles and become centred. We don't escape to the Himalayas; we move inwards to the point where nothing moves.

65

Learn to Remain Calm in all Situations

Life is nothing but an art of living. It all depends on how we look at everything and how we respond to situations. Every moment life is taking us into either happy or sad situations. And these are simply situations. An unintelligent person may turn these situations into problems while an intelligent person is one who can transform problems into situations. Intelligence is not born out of thinking but from moment-to-moment awareness that is meditation.

Osho talks about an incident in the life of Chuang Tzu, the great Taoist mystic of China. His wife had died and he was sitting in front of his hut playing on an instrument and singing. The emperor came to pay his respects. The emperor had rehearsed in his mind what to say to console Chuang Tzu. He thought of every good thing to console him, but the moment he saw Chuang Tzu, he became very uneasy. Chuang Tzu was singing. He looked very happy, when just in the morning his wife had died.

The emperor became uneasy and said, "Chuang Tzu, it is enough if you are not weeping, but the singing is too much. It is going too far!"

Chuang Tzu asked, "But why should I weep?"

66

The emperor said, "It seems you have not heard that your wife is dead."

Chuang Tzu said, "Of course, my wife is dead. Why should I weep? If she is dead, she is dead. And I never expected that she was going to live forever. You weep because you expect. I never expected that she was going to live forever. I always knew she was going to die any day, and this day it happened. This was going to happen any day. And any day is as good for death as any other, so why should I not sing? If I cannot sing when there is death, then I cannot sing in life, because life is a continuous death. They are one. The moment someone is born, death is born with him. And, moreover, the poor woman has lived so many years with me, so will you not allow me to sing a little in gratitude when she has left? She must go in peace, harmony, music and love. Why should I weep?"

Osho suggests: "Don't allow yourself to be miserable. Don't cooperate with misery; resist the temptation. It is very alluring — resist it! And try to be blissful in every state of mind. Whatsoever happens outside, don't allow it to disturb your bliss. Go on being blissful."

Be Natural and Follow the River Sutra

Why is there so much misery in life in spite of all the material comforts available to us? Why does man suffer endlessly? The enlightened sages have a simple answer to this difficult question: Be natural.

Osho presents a river *sutra* to regain the inner tranquillity that flows naturally within our being. He says: "Look at the river: Unconcerned with whatsoever is happening all around, it flows on in deep tranquillity, in deep calmness, undistracted by what is happening on the banks. Undistracted it moves on. It remains tuned to its own nature; it never goes out of its nature. It remains true to itself. Nothing distracts it and nothing calls it away, away from itself. Whatsoever happens in the world around, the river goes on being a river — true to itself, it goes on moving. Even if a war is going on, even if bombs are being dropped, whatsoever is happening, good or bad, the river remains true to itself. It goes on moving.

"Movement is its intrinsic nature. And tranquillity is a shadow when you are true to yourself."

Why is it so difficult to be authentic and true to oneself when the whole existence is comfortable to be so? Man wants to dominate others and become Alexander the Great. Nature does not suffer from such crazy ideas. An enlightened man follows the nature and lives in choiceless awareness. He drops all crazy ideas of conquering the world and dominating others. He becomes Master of his own self — a *swami*. He does not want to become anyone's carbon copy.

Happiness and harmony are possible to the original and natural. Just watch the flowers on the trees. The trees are true to themselves. No flower is trying in any way to imitate any other flower. There is no imitation, no competition and no jealousy. The red flower is just red, and tremendously happy in being red. It has never thought about being somebody else. Where has man been missing?

Osho points out: "Man misses his true nature because of desire, imitation, jealousy, competition. Man is the only being on earth who is not true to himself, whose river is not in tune with itself; who is always moving somewhere else; who is always looking at somebody else; who is always trying to be somebody else. That's the misery, the calamity. You can be only yourself. There is no other possibility; it simply does not exist. The sooner you understand it, the better. You cannot be a Buddha, you cannot be a Jesus, and there is no need. You can be only yourself."

Krishna: The Centre of the Cyclone

Lord Krishna is worshipped as a *paramyogi*, a *sannyasi* and a wise man. He is also a romantic lover, a shrewd warrior and a benevolent saviour — all in one! This may be the reason why he is worshipped by the Hindus as the *purnavtar*, a total incarnation of God on earth. No other incarnation of God is so much endowed with such diverse qualities as Krishna. All shades and colours of life — mischievous playfulness of a child, flirtatious romance of young man and ultimate maturity of a wise old man — meet in Krishna and they create a wide spectrum of colours, that have been attracting all kinds of artists, dancers, musicians, poets, writers and other creative people. The very meaning of his name Krishna is the element that attracts and pulls. Krishna is a magnetic force.

He is a perfect example of *mahadhyani* — greatest meditator — who is equally comfortable and fully centred when he is surrounded by his 16,000 pretty *gopis* and particularly when he is in the middle of an epic war. He is totally relaxed and playful in all these extreme situations and takes life as a cosmic *leela*, an ultimate dance of existence, which the poets have described as *raas*.

Osho says: "This word *raas* is very beautiful: It means the divine celebration, the divine dance. In this interplay of energies, which is *raas*, Krishna and his milkmaids cease to be individuals; they move as pure energies. And this dance of male and female energies together brings deep contentment and bliss; it turns into an outpouring of joy and bliss. Rising from Krishna's *raas* this bliss expands and permeates every fibre of the universe. Although Krishna and his girlfriends are no more with us as people, the moon and the stars under which they danced together are still with us, and so are the trees and the earth and the sky that were once so drunk with the bliss of the *raas*. Although millennia have passed, the vibes of the *maharaas* are still with us."

Osho adds, "If someone goes to dance on the grounds where Krishna once danced with his *gopis,* he can hear the echoes of the *maharaas*. If someone plays a flute near the hills that in the past echoed with the music of Krishna's flute, he can hear those hills echoing it, everlastingly. In my view, *raas* symbolises the outpouring of the primeval energy as it is divided between man and woman. And if we accept this definition, the *raas* is as relevant today as it was in the times of Krishna. Then it is everlastingly relevant."

Laughter, Hugs and Real Bliss

73

Celebrate aloneness, celebrate your pure space, and great song will arise in your heart. And it will be a song of awareness, it will be a song of meditation. It will be a song of an alone bird calling in the distance — not calling to somebody in particular, but just calling because the heart is full and wants to call, because the cloud is full and wants to rain, because the flower is full and the petals open and the fragrance is released... unaddressed. Let your aloneness become a dance.

—Osho

Hugs are for Free!

Several books have been written on the benefits of hugging. In recent times this human practice called hugging has evolved into a therapy. Marcia, a well-known Hug therapist, recommends four hugs a day for survival, eight hugs a day for maintenance and twelve hugs a day for growth.

Life does not believe in such arithmetic, though it is probably true that every human being needs a certain amount of touch and a certain number of hugs. The child may need more hugs than a grown-up. But then, not everybody grows up with the same speed, so in some cases a seemingly grown-up person may need more hugs than a child.

Our society does not recognise this human need and its response to this need is hardly sympathetic. No wonder then that it continues to suffer. People are not open to this human emotion though privately everyone loves to love and be loved in return. So the hugs have become very limited to occurring only between close relationships. There may be some lukewarm hugging between friends, which is not very nourishing. One needs more than that. What is then the alternative? Hug a tree! It won't get you into any trouble. And make it into a meditation.

Hugging a tree is an ancient technique of meditation that can be found in the *Vigyana Bhairav Tantra*, one of the oldest meditation manuals in existence, and composed in Sanskrit. Here is what Osho says on the subject of hugging a tree for meditation: "Leave one hour aside every day for a prayerful state of mind, and don't make your prayer a verbal affair. Make it a feeling thing. Rather than talking with the head, feel it. Go and touch the tree, hug the tree, kiss the tree; close your eyes and be with the tree as if you are with your beloved. Feel it. And soon you will come to a deep understanding of what it means to put the self aside, of what it means to become the other." Yes, and women can do it just as well as men. More on this can be found in *The Book of the Secrets* by Osho.

Osho suggests: "Sitting by the tree, just close your eyes, feel the tree. Hug the tree, just be one with it, as if you are with your beloved. And sometimes... and it is not predictable; I cannot say that it will happen each time. Only once in a while it will happen — because it has to happen in spite of you, that's why only once in a while."

Have you ever said 'hello' to a tree? Try it, and one day you will be surprised: The tree also says 'hello' in its tongue, in its own language. Hug a tree, and a day will come soon when you will feel that it was not only you who was hugging the tree — the tree was responding; you were also hugged by the tree, although the tree has no hands. But it has its own way of expressing its joy, its sadness, its anger, its fear.

Hug a tree and relax into it. Feel its green shape rushing into your being.

Laughter is made into a Film!

Osho says: "My definition of man is that man is the laughing animal. No computer laughs, no ant laughs, no bee laughs. If you come across a dog laughing you will be so scared! Or a buffalo suddenly laughs, you may have a heart attack. It is only man who can laugh, it is the highest peak of growth."

Laughter is also a spiritual quality, beneficial to the body, mind and soul. And once and for all, medical science has recently announced that laughter is good for health. Psychologically and spiritually it was always an established fact that laughter is good for health. Now it has been proven scientifically that genuine laughter increases endorphins — scientists describe these endorphins, as "little thingies in your brain that make you feel happy."

The report added, "Laughter 'massages' internal organs. This can aid in digestion and improve the flow of blood throughout the body. When you laugh the blood circulation in the body improves. For all body organs including the mind, this acts as an elixir. You can think more clearly, be more creative and solve problems better."

There are two ways to bring laughter to your life. First is to start your day with laughter meditation and the second thing is to get everybody in the office together and share a joke as morning prayer and then begin your office work. You will certainly have a better atmosphere in the office.

Osho has given some instructions for daily laughter meditation: "Every morning upon waking, before opening your eyes, stretch like a cat. Stretch every fibre of your body. After three or four minutes, with eyes still closed, begin to laugh. At first you will be doing it, but soon the sound of your attempt will cause genuine laughter. Lose yourself in laughter. It may take several days before it really happens, for we are so unaccustomed to the phenomenon. But before long it will be spontaneous and will change the whole nature of your day."

Wishing you a very healthy start for your day! And remember to share this health tonic with all without any discrimination. In the world of Osho, laughter is very sacred; it is like a daily prayer. And Osho world does not claim any copyright over it. Spread laughter and heal yourself and the world.

People living nine to five — or even more hours of office life are mostly a bored lot. If we look at them by the end of the day, we find them dull and comatose, as if the whole life has been sucked out from their being.

This boredom is a universal calamity that afflicts all human beings. People seek all kinds of entertainment and still remain affected with this malady. It is very rare to find freshness in people's lives because they don't live a life full of good cheer, joy and ecstasy. Work feels more like a burden than an enjoyable responsibility and sucks all the juice. It is so because the people don't live a life of meditation. With meditation work becomes art and ultimately worship. Then it transforms into a real source of joy.

Osho explains: "The first thing: A meditative mind always lives in the new, in the fresh. The whole existence is newly born — as fresh as a dew drop, as fresh as a leaf coming out in the spring. It is just like the eyes of a newborn babe: Everything is fresh, clear, with no dust on it. This is the first thing to be felt. If you look at the world and feel everything is old, it shows you are not meditative. When you feel everything is old, it shows you have an old mind, a rotten mind. If your mind is fresh, the world is fresh. The world is not the question, the mirror is the question. If there is dust on the mirror the world is old; if there is no dust on the mirror how can the world be old? If things get old, you will live in boredom; everybody lives in boredom; everybody is bored to death.

"Look at people's faces. They carry life as a burden — boring, with no meaning. It seems that everything is just a nightmare, a very cruel joke, that somebody is playing a trick, torturing them. Life is not a celebration, it cannot be. With a mind burdened by memory life cannot be a celebration. Even if you laugh, your laughter carries boredom. Look at people laughing: They laugh with an effort. Their laugh may be just to be mannerly; their laugh may be just etiquette."

People have forgotten how to have a hearty laugh. And laughter is exclusively a human quality.

Say 'Yes' to Life and Laugh Along

To be a really a religious person is something positive, and means saying 'yes' to life. Along with a yes, if we add laughter, then life takes on a totally new dimension.

Life follows two basic laws. One is the law of gravitation and the other is that of levitation. We can call it grace — the transcendental dimension of meditation. Gravitation keeps us in bondage while the law of levitation gives us freedom. This dimension is known to the mystics and the scientists of the inner world and they live a life of grace.

Osho talks about Zarathustra, who is known as the Laughing Prophet. His most famous statement condemns seriousness as a sin and appreciates laughter as a prayer. He says: "What has been the greatest sin here on earth? Was it not the saying, 'Woe to those who laugh'!"

For centuries, religious people have remained God-fearing and that has made them very serious. God has been understood by them as somebody above in the heaven who is going to punish us and throw us into hell if we enjoy the simple pleasures of life. This approach has created limitless misery in human life.

People have become incapable of enjoying life. They have

become life-negative. Zarasthustra and Osho did not agree with this approach and taught us to be life-affirmative. They said: "Live more, love more, and laugh more."

Talking about Zarasthustra, Osho says: "Laughter brings your energy back to you. Every fibre of your being becomes alive, and every cell of your being starts dancing. Zarathustra is right when he says that the greatest sin against man done on the earth is that he has been prohibited from laughing. The implications are deep, because when you are prohibited from laughing certainly you are prohibited from being joyous, you are prohibited from singing a song of celebration, you are prohibited from dancing just out of sheer blissfulness.

"By prohibiting laughter, all that is beautiful in life, all that makes life livable and lovable, all that gives meaning to life is destroyed. It is the ugliest strategy used against man. Seriousness is a sin. And remember, seriousness does not mean sincerity —sincerity is altogether a different phenomenon. A serious man cannot laugh, cannot dance, cannot play. He is always controlling himself; he has been brought up in such a way that he has become a jailer to himself. The sincere man can laugh, dance and rejoice sincerely. Sincerity has nothing to do with seriousness. Seriousness is simply sickness of the soul, and only sick souls can be converted into slaves."

Unburden Yourself with Laughter

Gautam Buddha made a profound statement: "Be a light unto yourself". To this, Osho adds another: "Be a joke unto yourself". Osho would say: "I have to tell jokes because you are all religious people; you tend to be serious. I have to tickle you sometimes so that you can forget your religiousness, your philosophies, theories, systems, and fall down to earth."

Osho has seen that in spontaneous laughter the noise of the mind stops for a few precious moments, allowing us to experience mindlessness or meditation, however fleetingly.

The seriousness of 'religious' people, however, is heavy on the human heart. It creates guilt in people: When you laugh, you feel you are doing something wrong. *Laughter* is good in a movie hall, but not in a church or temple.

Osho says: "I declare laughter to be the highest religious quality. And if we can decide that every year, for one hour, at a certain date, at a certain time, the whole world will *laugh* (together), it will help to dispel darkness, violence and stupidities — because laughter is a unique human characteristic... It can relax you, it can make you feel light, it can make your world a beautiful experience. It can change everything in your life. Laughter can make life worth living, something to be grateful for.

"German thinker Count Keyserling wrote that health is unreligious. But an ill person is desireless not because he has become desireless but because he is weak. A healthy person will laugh; he would like to enjoy, be merry — he cannot be sad.

"But 'religious' persons tell you to go on a fast, suppress your body, torture yourself. Laughter comes out of health. It's an overflowing energy. That's why children can laugh and their laughter is total. Their whole body is involved in it when they laugh; you can see their toes laughing."

Laughter, according to Osho, is multi-dimensional. When you laugh, your body, mind and your being laugh in unison. Distinctions, divisions and the schizophrenic personality disappear. That's why Osho introduced laughter to religion. Seriousness is of the ego whereas laughter is egolessness.

Religion cannot be anything other than a celebration of life. The serious person is handicapped; he creates barriers. He cannot dance, sing or celebrate. He becomes desert-like. And if you are a desert, you can go on thinking and pretending that you are religious but you are not.

You may be sectarian, but not religious. You believe in something, but you don't know anything. A man burdened by theories becomes serious. A man who is unburdened starts laughing.

The whole play of existence is so beautiful that laughter can be the only response to it. Only laughter can be the real prayer of gratitude. Osho talks about a great Zen Master, Hotei who was known in Japan as the 'Laughing Buddha'.

Osho says: "Hotei is tremendously significant... more people should be like Hotei; more temples should be full of laughter, dancing and singing. If seriousness is lost, nothing is lost, in fact, one becomes more healthy and whole. But if laughter is lost, everything is lost. Suddenly you lose the festivity of your being; you become colourless, monotonous, in a way, dead. Then your energy is not streaming any more."

But to understand Hotei you will have to be in that festive dimension. If you are too much burdened with theories, concepts, notions, ideologies, theologies, philosophies, you will not be able to realise the significance of Hotei.

Osho warns that taking man's laughter away from him is taking his very life away; it is a form of spiritual castration.

83

Your Best Medicine

"Start every New Year on a note of cheerful laughter," suggests Osho. It keeps the ego at bay and invites the cosmos to join in.

My approach towards life is that of laughter. And laughter contains love, joy and gratitude. Laughter contains tremendous thankfulness towards God. When you are really in deep belly laughter, your ego disappears.

It happens rarely in any other activity, but in laughter it is bound to happen. If the laughter is total, ego cannot exist; nothing kills ego like laughter.

That's why egoists are serious. Ego can exist only in seriousness; ego lives, feeds on seriousness. And serious people are dangerous.

We have to destroy all kinds of seriousness in the world. Temples should be full of laughter, song, dance and celebration. That's how trees, stars, rivers and oceans are. The whole existence, except man, is in a non-serious state; only man seems to be serious.

No child is born serious, remember, but we destroy a child's innocence. His qualities of wonder and awe. We destroy his laughter and everything beautiful and valuable.

Instead we give him a load to carry — of knowledge, of theology, of philosophy. The more he becomes educated, the more he loses his sense of humour. He starts living through his knowledge. And because he starts to know so much that awe and sense of wonder are lost. The laughter I am teaching is something that will destroy you completely. It is a crucifixion.

But only after destruction is there creation. Only from chaos are stars born. Only after crucifixion is there resurrection.

No, you will not be able to survive this laughter. If you really allow it, you will be drowned by it. You will disappear and only laughter will remain.

If you laugh then laughter is not total. When there is only laughter and you are not, then it is total. And only then have you heard God's joke.

Yes, this whole cosmos is a joke. Hindus call it *leela*. It is a joke, it is a play. And the day you understand, you start laughing. That laughter never stops. It spreads all over the cosmos.

Laughter is prayer.

If you can laugh, you have learnt to pray. Don't be serious. Serious people can never be religious. Only a person who can laugh, not only at others but at himself, can be religious.

A person who can laugh absolutely, who sees the ridiculousness at the game of life, becomes enlightened in that laughter.

I teach you life, love. I teach you how to sing and dance. To transform life into a carnival of delight.

Even if you cry and weep, your tears should have the quality of laughter in them. They should come dancing and singing; they should not be tears of sadness and misery.

To Live with Nature is to Live with God

Why do people go to a temple? The answer is obvious: To find peace, to sit and meditate and to feel the energy of those who have meditated there earlier.

But today, most of the traditional temples have become centres of trade and politics. Regular prayers may be offered here, but these prayers are formal and out of a fear of God. There's no innocence in these prayers. In such an atmosphere polluted with materialism and politics, meditation is not possible.

If we are really interested in meditation and prayer, we need to look for a different kind of temple and one that is not man-made.

The good news is that such unpolluted temples of love still exist. You will find them in nature. Go and sit under a tree, breathe and meditate and you will be filled with love-prayer.

The tree always gives life-energy. It will never ask you about your religion or caste. You can hug a tree and you will feel its heart beat. And at the same time you will also feel your own heart beat.

But when you hug fellow human beings, you will not have the same feelings because nobody nowadays hugs anyone unconditionally. The tree is a temple of love, as it always gives.

Go to the mountains or the sea and sit in the open spaces. While you listen to the sound of mountains, streams, you will automatically start meditating. Meditation needs a certain kind of an atmosphere, a space for the soul, where it can fly high in the sky. And that's possible only in nature.

Talking about the songs of the mystic saint Kabir, Osho says: "To live with nature is to live with God in an indirect way, because nature reflects God in a-thousand-and-one ways. The trees and the call of the cuckoo and the winds in the pine trees and the rivers moving towards the ocean and the proud mountains standing in the sun and the starry night, and it is impossible not to be reminded of some invisible hand. The ocean heaves, breathes; the whole existence is a growing phenomenon. It is not dead, it cannot be dead.

"Everything is growing. Because of this growing experience, man has remained constantly aware of some invisible, mysterious force behind it all. That force is called God. God is not a person, but just a presence. Still when you go deep into the Himalayas, you again start feeling a kind of reverence, awe, wonder. Again you start feeling something that was very easily available to the primitive man."

Here & Now

Meditation makes you spacious, it cleanses all your senses. It makes your sensitivity so sharp that the smallest fragrance passing by your side, and you will immediately get it. Just a small sound, even the sound of silence, will be heard so loudly and so clear.

We are living in trivia, and all that is great in existence we are missing. Only a man of no-mind, a man of enlightenment, knows what beauty is, what joy is, what ecstasy is. And the moment you know what ecstasy is, you know you don't need any God, you don't need any commandment, you don't need any discipline. Everything comes out of your no-mind, fresh. You live for the first time in freedom without bondage.

—Osho

Live for Today

The simplest definition of enlightenment that Osho offers was to live one's life here and now: This moment is all. He says: "You never have two moments together in your hands; only one single moment. It is such a small moment that there is no space for thinking to move, no space for thoughts to exist. Either you can live it, or you can think. To live it is to be enlightened; to think is to miss."

Osho does not talk about enlightenment as a goal that you have to decide whether to accept it or not. He says: "Enlightenment is the realisation that we have only the present moment to live. The next moment is not certain — it may come, it may not come."

Jesus said to his disciples, "Look at the lilies in the field, how beautiful they are! Even the great Solomon was not so beautifully attired in all his grandeur as these poor lily flowers." And what is the secret? The secret is that they think not of the morrow. They live now; they live here. To live now is to be enlightened, to live here is to be enlightened, to be a lily is to be enlightened this very moment! Don't think about what I am saying. Don't think about it, just be here. This is the taste of enlightenment. And once you have tasted it, you will want to taste it more and more.

OSHO FRAGRANCE

Osho adds: "It will bring you, for the first time, real contentment, real blissfulness, authentic ecstasy." Once enlightenment gives you a taste of the real, you will see that all your pleasures, all your happinesses were simply the stuff dreams are made of; they were not real. And what has come now, has come forever.

That is the definition of the real: A contentment that comes and never leaves you again is real contentment. A contentment that comes and goes again is not contentment; it is simply a gap between two miseries. Let that be the definition. Anything that comes and never goes is reality.

Don't be bothered about the word 'enlightenment'. What you call it does not matter; you can call it illumination, you can call it blissfulness, you can call it self-realisation, you can call it actualisation of all your potentials — whatever you want to call it.

But remember one quality, that it knows only a beginning; it knows no end.

The Bliss of Eternal Now

Our mind is a very strange mechanism. It is an unstoppable manufacturer of thoughts which are either of the past or the future. And they are all a source of tensions — the past pulls us backwards while the future pulls us forward. The mind does not know how to remain in the present moment.

Actually, the present is not a tense, though it exists in our language. The present is a space of no tenses, no tension between the past and future tenses. It is a space of eternal now. Meditation takes place in this space.

A meditator gets momentary flashes in this space in the beginning and they are such a joy, while a *siddha* or an enlightened one becomes permanently settled in such a space of eternal now. When Jesus Christ was asked the definition of the kingdom of God, he replied: "In my kingdom of God, there shall be time no longer." This is a unique definition, but very significant. The Buddhists, Hindus, Jains and Christians may have their ideological differences about all other dimensions of their religions, but on the description of *nirvana*, *moksha*, self-realisation or kingdom of God, they all seem to agree.

Osho elaborates on the phenomenon of past, present, future

and timelessness: "And when yesterdays are gone and tomorrows are gone, where is today? It exists between the two. If both the banks have disappeared, the bridge will disappear. Chunk by chunk, in three pieces, time dissolves: First the past, then the future, and finally the present. Then you are left with no time; a state of timelessness. And this, Buddha says, is *nirvana*. To experience timelessness is to experience deathlessness. To experience timelessness is to experience that which really is. It is neither past nor present nor future; it simply is. It cannot be confined to any compartment, into any category; it cannot be categorised. You simply experience each moment with tremendous peace and silence and joy. And each moment becomes fragrant and alive! Each moment becomes such a benediction that it is impossible to imagine or describe it. One has to know it to know it; there is no other way. It is not expressible; it is not explainable. It is the greatest mystery...Jesus will call it the kingdom of God; that is a positive way of describing it. And the Buddha calls it a state of cessation — all has ceased."

Correct Breathing can Help Change Lives

It is the knack of being in the 'here and now' rather than in the 'there and then' which adds zest to our dull life.

One meditation method which has been effective for the last 10,000 years is the watching of one's breath. This method has never failed simply because it brings our entire consciousness in the moment. Meditation also means the art of being in the moment — no past, no future, just in this moment.

When we pray or chant a *mantra*, our mind can wander off in all directions. Thinking continues. Calculations go on. We may start dreaming or having an inner dialogue with our wife or girlfriend, friend or enemy. It does not matter with whom — we may start talking with the Almighty God of our own imagination.

We may create any hallucination. Everything that our mind takes us to the past or the future. And what brings us back in the moment? The breathing.

We cannot breathe in the past or the future. It is simply impossible. When we breathe, our thinking also stops because the breathing needs all the attention. You cannot divide the attention.

OSHO FRAGRANCE

Breath generates a certain amount of energy in the body that has its own effect. In certain meditation methods, especially devised by Osho for the modern man, vigorous breathing takes place. Such methods are even better than simple methods of watching the breath.

Such methods bring deeper relaxation and when you relax, you can watch your breath passively and naturally and continue to remain in the moment. In Vipassana, one goes inward with the breath consciously and comes out with it consciously. There's no time gap in between. You are not thinking of exhaling when you are inhaling. You are not thinking of inhaling when you are exhaling. Try this method and see what happens to you in this process. Go on to the terrace or under a tree or some other solitary place where there is no possibility of any interference.

For some time, as long as you feel, breathe vigorously — bring all your energy to exhaling and inhaling. The moment will come naturally when you will feel like sitting down or just standing or you may even want to lie down. Do that.

Then watch your breath going in and coming out. You will feel the deepest rest and total relaxation, at the same time a glimpse of meditation. With such techniques, you can always find your own rhythm and time limit.

Celebrate Love

In love, you connect with the other; in meditation, you connect with yourself. Both are enriching. Unless a love is based in deep meditation, it will be superficial. It will never be intimate, it will not have any profundity. It will not bring bliss to you; it will bring only agonies, it will never bring ecstasy. The love has to be based on meditation. And a meditation that is against love, anti-love, will be a dry desert, a wasteland. No flower will ever bloom there.

—Osho

Love: Fly High into an Open Sky

We all love to be loved. Life without love seems to be totally meaningless. Love comes as a fresh breeze that opens our hearts and raises our consciousness. We open our wings like free birds and fly high into the sky.

Love brings a dance to our ordinary walk. We walk as if we are not walking — we start flying. The gravitational phenomenon that pulls us down starts losing its grip and we enter into the realm of grace that pulls us upward. Love is an ultimate taste of freedom. This freedom is very unique — it is freedom not only from others but from oneself also. Love is just a state of egolessness.

Osho tells a beautiful anecdote. There was a very well-known poem by the Sufi poet Rumi. The lover went and knocked at the door of the beloved. A voice asked, "Who is it?"

He said, "Open the door. It is I."

There was no answer, all was silent within. The lover knocked again. He called out again and again, "Open the door. It is I, your lover," but there was no response.

98

Finally a voice came from within, "Two cannot be contained in this house. This is the house of love; it cannot accommodate two." Then again there was silence.

The lover turned back. He wandered for years in the jungles. He undertook many fasts and practices; he performed many rites and holy works. He purified himself and thus cleansed his mind. He became more aware; he began to understand the conditions.

After many, many years he returned once again and knocked at the door. The same question came from within, "Who is it?"

But this time the answer that came from outside was, "You alone are."

And, Rumi says, the door was opened.

If you go to the gates of God as somebody, then even if you appear as a *sannyasin*, a renunciate, a wise man, whatever, you will fail. The gate opens only for those who are nothing, nobody, who have annihilated their selves totally.

In ordinary life also, love opens its doors only when you are not, when you are completely merged in the other and the voice of 'I' has stopped. Then when this 'I' becomes less important than you, and when 'you' becomes your whole life, then you are capable of destroying yourself for the beloved; you willingly and happily enter into death. Then only does love blossom. In everyday life we thus get a glimpse of the one when two are no more.

Love opens its doors only when you are completely merged in the other and the voice of 'I' has stopped.

LOVE: FLY HIGH INTO AN OPEN SKY

"When the ultimate love arises, there should remain no sign of you; your name, your designation, your very self should turn to dust. Only when you annihilate yourself completely can this happen. Remember the words of Jesus: He who saves himself will be lost; he who loses himself will be saved. In His kingdom he who destroys himself attains everything and he who saves himself loses everything," (*Osho: The True Name*).

In another discourse, Osho illustrates true love: Love gives you freedom to be yourself, helps you to be yourself.

Even if it goes against his own interest, still a loving person will suffer himself rather than make the loved one suffer.

Another ancient story...

A woman loved her husband, but the husband never paid any attention to her. He was in love with a prostitute, knowing perfectly well that prostitutes don't love — because there were many other customers. He was only a customer, not a lover. And in his life he had seen that the day the customer's money is finished, the prostitute's door is closed for that man.

He had destroyed his health, he had destroyed his money, now he was dying. Just as he was dying, his wife asked him, "If you have any last wish so that you can die contented..."

He said, "Yes, I have a wish, but I am ashamed to say it to you."

"I love you as you are."

She said, "Don't be ashamed. This is not the time to be ashamed. I love you as you are — there is no question of feeling ashamed."

He said, "My only wish is to see the prostitute just once more before I die."

The woman said, "There is no problem."

He had lost all their money; there was no money in the house. She had to carry the dying man on her shoulders to the prostitute's house. She knocked on the door.

The prostitute opened the door and could not believe it. She said, "Am I hallucinating? Is this real? You are the wife of the man..."

The wife said, "Yes, I am the wife and also the lover of the man."

The prostitute said, "Then why have you brought him here? He destroyed your life, he spent all your money and he was mad after me. And for me, once the money is finished, all relationship is finished. He was only a customer. This is a marketplace and he knows it. You are a strange woman!"

She said, "But this was his dying wish. He wanted to see you, and I love him so much that I could not say 'no'. In his happiness is my happiness, and if he can die contented I will feel I have fulfilled my duty, my love."

No complaint about the man, about his whole behaviour. No jealousy against the woman. Love knows no jealousy, love knows no complaint. Love is a deep understanding.

You love someone — that does not mean that the other should love you also. It is not a contract. Try to understand the meaning of love. And you will not be able to understand the meaning of love by your so-called love affairs.

Strangely enough, you will understand the meaning of love by going deep into meditation, by becoming more silent, more together, more at ease. You will start radiating a certain energy. You will become loving, and you will know the beautiful qualities of love.

Love Nourishes Body, Soul

Love is the most spiritual experience in our life, and it is nourishment for our body, mind and soul.

We come to the world, and we don't know why we came. We will die one day and death will come unannounced. So birth and death is not our choice.

Between this birth and death, love is the only phenomenon we have some choice about. Only this choice of love gives us a sense of freedom in our life.

But unfortunately we live it so unconsciously that even our love becomes reduced to attachment or bondage, and then love becomes misery.

The mystic Mirdad said, "Love is the only freedom from attachment. When you love everything, you are attached to nothing." Loving everything and being attached to nothing simply means the quality of being loving. Love becomes our fragrance.

And later Mirdad added, "Man made prisoner by the love of a woman and vice versa are equally unfit for freedom's precious crown. But man and woman made as one by love, inseparable, indistinguishable, are verily entitled to the prize."

Whether it is man-woman relationship or any other relationship, love is much more than a relationship; it is a moment-to-moment process of relating consciously.

Be Real and Love Yourself

What is the most essential thing for the seeker on the path? What is his goal? What should he pursue to attain bliss and contentment? The first and foremost thing is this *mantra*: "Be yourself."

The social environment that surrounds us expects us always to live in a particular way that suits its structure and the whole package of investment in it. And there's not so much regard for the individual, his original self and his freedom. The individual is sacrificed to something very artificial and superficial. Almost every child is made to grow so only that he loses his real self in his growth process. One becomes too much concerned about, even scared of others' opinions about oneself, keeps seeking approval from others and does not give love and respect to oneself. This is the surest way to become sad and miserable. This calamity happens to each child while he is growing to become a part of society.

Osho suggests that the first thing is to love oneself. "This can become the foundation of a radical transformation. Don't be afraid of loving yourself. Love totally, and you will be surprised; the day you can get rid of all self-condemnation, self-disrespect, the day you can get rid of the idea of original sin, the day you can think of yourself as worthy and loved by God, will be a day of great blessing.... And a person who loves himself can easily become meditative, because meditation means being with yourself. If you hate yourself — as you do, as you have been told to do, and you have been following it religiously — if you hate yourself, how can you be with yourself? And meditation is nothing but enjoying your beautiful aloneness, celebrating yourself; that's what meditation is all about."

If you are lost too much in social formalities and moralities and have become fake, you need to come back home urgently and be natural and spontaneous. Be real! And you would become blissful and contented.

Love is Real Nourishment

Relationships are always a big issue in life — the only one. We spend life thinking and worrying on how to relate with others, how deeply or superficially we should involve ourselves with them. We often get into all kinds of entanglements. And each relationship promises pleasure in the beginning, then turns sour. Some create insecurity, others make us dependent.

Some relationships appear so beautiful that we don't want to lose them and become possessive. Then comes bondage leading to suffering and misery. Relationships create extreme reactions in our being — either we become possessive or start escaping. And these extreme situations are not healthy and harmonious. They have nothing much to do with love — they are weaknesses, dependence on others. They keep our mind, heart and emotions in turmoil. They are not nourishing.

Love is real nourishment but it has nothing much to do with the way we relate with people. Love is a pure joy but these relationships suck our life and leave us in anguish. What is the way then? How to go beyond bondage and misery?

Osho guides us: "My vision of a real humanity is of pure

individuals relating to each other but not tied in any relationship. They will be loving to each other but not be possessive. They will be sharing with all their joys and blessings, but never even in their dreams thinking of dominating, thinking of enslaving the other."

My vision of real humanity is of a world consisting not of families, nations or races, but individuals.

He says: "Going beyond needs, demands, desires, love becomes a soft sharing, great understanding. When you understand yourself, that day you have understood the whole of humanity. Then nobody can make you miserable..."

108

Celebrate to Dispel Inner Darkness

How do you welcome a new year? Is there anything new about the year other than that we lost one year of our life and became a year older?

This is true but a depressing way of looking at the arrival of a new year. This is not the way one should live one's life. To really welcome the arrival of the new year, one has to learn the art of living each moment of one's life with a freshness. And in Osho's view, "squeezing the juice of life from each moment."

Life does not come in days, weeks, months or years. It actually comes to us each moment. Thus, each moment has to be welcomed fully as it comes. Only then we will be really capable of celebrating new year. This is a right approach to all of our celebrations.

Celebration should be a way of life and should not be postponed to certain dates of the calendar, though it is also equally meaningful to celebrate birthdays of those whom we love and adore, such as our relatives and friends, enlightened mystics, masters, *sadgurus* and sages. What is really important is to celebrate and dispel darkness and dullness from our lives. Celebrations transform our life of routine and boredom into rejuvenation and rejoicing. Life is not life if we are not really alive and throbbing. Celebration is a pulsation of life.

The tragedy is that except human beings, the whole of creation is always celebrating. Nature celebrates without any purpose or reason. In spite of all the ravages that mankind has been unleashing on nature, it continues to produce more foliage and flowers, and keeps sharing with all. Nature is not miserly, that's why it has abundance to share.

Osho says, "Nature is a spendthrift. Where one flower is needed it produces millions. One tree will produce... look at the *Gulmohar*, millions of seeds are ready. They will all fall down and a few may become trees. Why so many seeds? God is not a miser. If you ask for one, he gives millions. Just ask! Jesus has said, 'Knock and the doors shall be opened unto you, ask and it shall be given.' Remember, if you ask for one, millions will be given."

Man is miserly, and his miserliness is his real misery. Miserly people are incapable of trusting life and that's why life does not open its treasures to them.

Ishwar is one of the names of God; whatever comes from God is called *aishwarya*. God gives in abundance and this abundance can be shared with one and all. The more we share the more we feel natural and godly.

Creativity is the Path to Love Life

L ove is an infinite source of creativity. Osho has a beautiful Sufi story to tell in this connection. A great emperor used to go around the town every day early in the morning. It was a beautiful exercise for him and also an experience to see how the city was growing, how his capital was becoming more beautiful.

He had a dream to make it the most beautiful place on earth. But he was always puzzled. And he always stopped his horse and watched an old man, who must have been 120-years old. This man was always working in the garden, sowing seeds, watering trees — trees which would take hundreds of years to reach their youth and then live for four thousand years. He was left puzzled: For whom was this old man sowing these seeds? He will never be able to see the fruits and the flowers. One day, when he could no longer resist his temptation, he asked the old man: "I want to know for whom you are sowing these seeds? These trees will grow when you are no longer here."

The old man laughed and said, "If this had been the logic of my forefathers, then I would not have been able to get fruits and flowers and this beautiful garden. I am a gardener for generations — my father and my forefathers planted seeds, I have eaten the fruit. What about my children? What about my children's children? If they too had the same views like you do, then there would have been no garden. People come from distant places to see this place because I have trees that are thousands of years old. I am simply doing whatever I can out of gratitude.

"And as far as sowing of seeds is concerned, it gives me immense joy when I see green leaves sprouting during spring. It makes me forget how old I am. I have remained young because I have continued to be creative. Death takes away people who become useless; perhaps that why I have lived so long, and still I am young. Death is compassionate to me because I am keeping pace with existence."

Osho concludes that the only way to live life is to create more life. "Don't leave this earth unless you have made it a little better — this is the only religion that I know of. I teach you the religion of creativity. And by creating more life, you will be transformed because one who can create life has already become part of God, of godliness."

112

To be in Romance with Life is Religion

Jesus says: 'God is love.' Osho says: 'Love is God.'

Love is the most essential feeling that is central to our life. Love is the nucleus of our existence. It is hard to imagine that one can be religious without being loving. Anybody who thinks love has nothing to do with religion is not in tune with the heart and spirit of life.

Love becomes ultimate bliss when it is universal. Love becomes imprisonment and misery when it starts clinging and is possessive. On such a level it becomes one with godliness.

Commenting on the statements of Jesus, Osho says: "God is creativity." Or, if you allow me to say it, I would like to say that God is the very existence itself. God is life, God is love. God is this very world. Don't create a division, don't create a dualism. Only then can you revere life. Whenever you see life anywhere — a seed sprouting, a tree flowering, stars moving, a river flowing, a child laughing — remember God is near you.

When a child laughs, look at the laughter. Enter into it. You have entered the very temple. When the river flows, watch lovingly. Be one with its flow; be in a deep reverence. For the Hindus all their rivers are goddesses while their hills are the deities.

They have made the earth holy. It is one of the most beautiful things that has ever happened in human consciousness. Hindus call River Ganges: Mother. This is reverence for life. Hills, they call gods. This is reverence for life. They worship trees. Those who have become intellectually sophisticated think Hindus are stupid, superstitious people, but they are not. The tree is not the thing. When they are worshipping a tree or a river, they are worshipping life.

A tree is more alive than any temple, than any church; a river is more alive than any mosque. The stone idols in your temples are dead; a tree is more alive.

You may be superstitious, but the person who is worshipping a tree is not. He may not be aware of what he is doing, but a deep reverence for life in all its forms is there; a deep respect.

A really religious person is in love with life. This is a higher kind of romance. And to be in romance with life is religion.

Place at God's Feet Your Flowers of Feelings

The Baul mystics of Bengal always sing songs of love, full of reverence for the earth. They are deeply in love with life on earth and do not promise any imaginary heaven in the sky. They are the real people who sing real songs.

In one of the poems a Baul mystic sings:

Commit yourself to the earth
while on the earth, my heart
if you wish to attain
the unattainable man.

The 'unattainable man' means the God within us, who is the essential man. The Bengali name is *adhar manush*. The unattainable man is not to be attained somewhere in the Himalayas or the heavens but within us, in the deepest core of our being. It is to be discovered in our meditation, and this process of meditation need not be something serious and grim. In fact, it is an outpouring of our gratefulness to the earth and the whole of existence. All the elements of this existence have created us. We have no reason to feel egoistic as we are not in any way separate from this existence. We are the organic manifestation of this existence. To feel one with it, we simply need to come down from the clouds of our head to our heart and follow our feelings.

The Baul mystics sing:

Place at his feet your flowers of feeling
and the prayers of tears flooding your eyes.

Osho extolles the nature of these mystics and says: "They are real people. They say 'the flowers of feelings'. Ordinary flowers won't do. You can pick flowers from the trees and go to the God of your temple and put those flowers there, but the God is abstract, the flowers borrowed."

In fact, they were more in tune with God on the trees. You have not made them closer to God; you have killed them. The Bauls say, *'your flowers of feelings place at his feet'*, which means your love, compassion and understanding.

In *A Cup of Tea*, his most famous book of letters written to the seekers, Osho reveals: "The secret of all prayer and worship is hidden in the overflow of those tears. They are sacred. God fills the heart of those He blesses with tears of love, and what to say about the calamity of those whose hearts are filled instead with thorns of hate? Tears flowing in love are offerings of flowers at the feet of God and the eyes from which they flow are blessed with divine vision. Only eyes filled with love can see God. Love is the only energy that transcends the inertia of nature and takes one to the shores of ultimate awareness."

Maths and the Heart

One can live all the colours of love — the rainbow of love – but it is not easy to understand what this phenomenon is.

Osho explains this in one of his discourses compiled in *The Ancient Music in the Pines*. Love is illogical. Love is irrational. Love is life. Love comprehends all contradictions in it. Love is even capable of comprehending its opposite, hate.

117

You go on hating the same person you love. But love is bigger. In fact, if you really love, hate is not a distraction; on the contrary, it gives colour, spice. It makes the affair more colourful — like a rainbow.

Even hate is not the opposite for a loving heart. He can hate and continue loving. Love is so great that even hate can be allowed to have its say. Lovers become intimate enemies; they go on fighting.

In fact, if you ask expert analysts, they'll say when a couple stops fighting, love has also stopped. When a couple becomes indifferent to each other, love stops. If you still fight with your wife, husband, boyfriend or girlfriend, life is still running in it; it is still a live wire, still hot. Or else one settles into a sort of coldness, indifference.

Love is like wildlife — hence, Jesus's saying: 'God is love.' He means if you love, you will know many things which are qualities of God that he comprehends as opposites.

That even the devil is allowed to have his say. That the enemy is also a friend. That death is not against life but a part of it and life is a part of death.

The whole is bigger than all opposites, not just a total of opposites — it is more than the total. That is higher mathematics of the heart.

Of course, a man of love will look mad. He will look mad to you because you function from the head, he functions from the heart; the languages are totally different.

For example, Jesus was crucified. His enemies waited for him to cure them and were a little afraid. His friends were waiting for him to do miracles that would cause the enemies to fall dead.

And what did he do? A near mad thing. He prayed to God to forgive these people because they didn't know what they were doing.

This is the madness of love. It is unexpected of someone who is being killed to pray for the forgiveness of his persecutors because they don't know what they are doing. The are completely unconscious. Sleep-walkers.

Whatsoever they are doing is not their responsibility, because how can you throw responsibility on somebody who is asleep? They are unconscious – forgive them. This is the miracle that happened that day, but nobody could see the miracle; it was sheer madness.

Love's language is so foreign to the head. Head and heart

are farthest poles of reality.

There is no greater distance between any other two points, as there is between head and heart, reason and love, logic and life. If a person is mad because of love, his madness is not disease.

In fact, he is the only healthy person, the only holy person — because through his heart he has bridged with life.

Unconditional Love Brings Joy to All

All of us need to believe that we are loved and are lovable. We begin life secure in our mother's love, swaddled in our innocence. Love was never in question, but over time, we become increasingly unsure...

In *The Path to Love*, Deepak Chopra says that by bringing spirituality back into our relationships, we can discover a world of depth and meaning. He says: "You were created to be completely loved and to be completely lovable for your whole life."

The problems begin when we start taking love for granted and get possessive about life. We deny freedom and space to the people we love — our children, spouse, friend. Unknowingly, we start killing our love. And we create bondage for ourselves, too, when we curb the freedom of the person we love.

Osho says: "Freedom has a higher value than love." Love stifles and gets stifled when it encroaches upon the space of another. Love blossoms in the space of freedom, in breeziness. Once we realise the nature of true love, we no longer 'fall' in love — we actually 'rise' in love.

At this point love becomes unconditional. We give our love

and feel grateful to all those who receive it, because this way we unburden ourselves.

Osho says when the clouds are full of rain-water, they have to shower. It is their need. Similarly, when we become full of love, it is our need to give our love to one and all. Then we are not concerned whether or not we receive love in return. We simply enjoy giving.

Conditional love is attachment; it is bondage, so it is also an illusion. We say we want to be free but are we brave enough to be alone? We fear loneliness. We fear being unoccupied. We started out looking for love, but maybe we were really looking for attachment. Our need may have been an attachment all along. Love was the way to attain it, the bait.

Unconditional love will not become attachment. But the moment you say to your partner, "Love only me," you begin to possess her. And in possessing, you're making your lover into an object to be used.

Emmanuel Kant said that to treat another person as a means is an immoral act. In other words, if you see your lover as being there for your gratification, or to fulfil your sexual desires, or to provide something else for you, you're reducing your partner to an object.

You are in bondage — so inevitably, you'll eventually desire freedom. You will be bored by what you have and yearn for what you don't have. Or you could try to be free even while 'possessing' your partner, causing a struggle.

Osho says, "I want to be a free person, and yet I want you to be possessed by me; you want to retain your freedom and still possess me — this is the struggle... We must remain individuals and we must move as independent, free consciousness. We can come together, we can merge into each other, but no one can possess us. Then there is no bondage and then there is no attachment."

Love becomes a blessing, a real celebration when love breathes fresh air, free from possessiveness and jealousy. There should be no judgment, no blame, no expectations and no attempts to control.

The soul can grow only in freedom — and unconditional love provides freedom. Osho says: "My message is beyond biology and theology... Love is nothing but sharing of your consciousness with as many people as possible; not only with people, but with animals, trees, birds, clouds, stars."

Compassion is the Real Therapy

The unconditional love that flows between a mother and her children, or in any relationship, is the greatest therapy that heals all wounds. Such a love becomes a fragrance of compassion.

In the phenomenon of love, passion functions as the fire that can burn people; and compassion as a flame that can illuminate people's life. The whole journey of love is between passion and compassion. Passion is a very limited phenomenon, flowing only between a few relationships and gets exhausted very quickly, while compassion knows no limits; it is like a breeze.

Bodhidharma, Gautam Buddha's enlightened disciple, went to China. A man came to see him and said, "Master, according to your teachings, I meditate and I feel compassion for the whole universe — not only for men, but for animals, for rocks and rivers also. But there is one problem: I cannot feel compassion for my neighbour. Can you please tell me if I can exclude my neighbour from my compassion? I include the whole existence, known, unknown, but can I exclude my neighbour, because it is very difficult, impossible. I cannot feel compassion for him."

Bodhidharma is reported to have said, "Then forget about

meditation, because if compassion excludes anybody, then it is not really compassion."

Osho explains: "Compassion is all-inclusive, intrinsically all-inclusive. So if you cannot feel compassion for your neighbour, then forget all about meditation, because it has nothing to do with somebody in particular. It has something to do with your inner state. Be compassionate — unconditionally, undirected, unaddressed. Then you become a healing force in this world of misery."

Meditation is the magical alchemy that purifies passion and transforms it into compassion. The very touch of such a meditative person becomes therapeutic. Osho says: "Compassion is always therapeutic; whatsoever your level, it helps you. Compassion is love purified, so much so that you simply give and don't ask for anything in return."

Buddha used to say to his disciples, "After each meditation, be compassionate immediately, because when you meditate, love grows, the heart becomes full. After each meditation, feel compassion for the whole world so that you share your love and you release the energy into the atmosphere so that energy can be used by others."

He added: "I would also like to say to you that after each meditation, when you are celebrating, have compassion. Just feel that your energy should go and help people in whatsoever way they need it. Just release it!"

Meditation

Meditate on the rose flower as much as you can. Whenever you see a rose flower, sit by the side; have a little dialogue with the flower. First see the flower then close your eyes; see the flower in the heart. Visualise the heart opening like a rose flower. Soon it will become a great meditation for you and you will start opening with it. When you feel the opening of the heart there will be great joy.

—Osho

Meditation is the Key

"Every morning when I get up, the first thing I decide is: 'What do you want? Misery? Blisfulness? What are you going to choose today?' And it happens that I always choose blissfulness. It is my choice, it is my life," says Abdullah.

Our life is out of our own choice. Our birth though, was not our choice — it was a decision of our parents. They brought us into this world without consulting us or even seeking an approval from us.

How does this happen? How do we drop misery and choose peace and happiness?

The answer is: By being a master of oneself.

In India *sannyasins* are called Swami. Why? We call them so because they do not let anybody else or society decide about his life. A Swami makes his own decisions and lives according to his own set of rules. He moves in total freedom and takes all the responsibility about his life on himself. Such a life has its own risks. People may not respect him or may consider him anti-social. But this does not bother a true Swami as his bliss of freedom from slavery of the society is so gratifying that he can renounce the false coins of respectability and hypocrisy given by society. This is the real renunciation.

A *sannyasin* does not run away from the world or renounce the society but he drops all dependence on the society and its allurements, which come with golden fetters. He is like a bird on the wing, flying in the sky with two wings of freedom and wisdom. Out of his feeling of compassion and consciousness he does what he can for the society, but he never tries to fulfil anybody's expectations to gain respect and satisfy his ego.

Ego is the greatest bondage that imprisons consciousness of an individual. It is a trap of the unconscious mind to enslave the individual. A conscious person can always choose and attain freedom from misery. Meditation is the master key to unlock the chains of human misery.

Osho says : "Meditation brings two things. It brings wisdom, it brings freedom. These two flowers grow out of meditation. When you become silent, utterly silent, beyond the mind, two flowers bloom in you. One is of wisdom: You know what is and what is not. And the other is of freedom: You know now there are no more any limitations on you, either of time or of space. You become liberated. Meditation is the key to liberation, to freedom, to wisdom."

Before the dawn of the new millennium there were great expectations that it will usher in a new era of non-violence, peace and prosperity. This desire was bubbling in human hearts universally. The world celebrated the arrival of the new millennium to leave the past behind once and for all. But this did not happen. The past made a comeback with a big bang and unleashed the rein of terror and violence with all the fire of revengefulness. The new millennium made the depressing prophecies of despair and world war alive once again.

Once again Nostradamus and other prophets of doom sprang back to life and death started doing a *tandav* in front of our eyes. We are witnessing violence at our doorsteps, not so far, and around us. We were surrounded by it, bathed in it. We sleep with it every night and dream the nightmares of violence. It has become our breakfast, lunch and supper. We are in it. Now we are breathing it — inhaling it and exhaling it. Violence has become an inhuman facet of human life. Violence has entered deep in our unconscious, so much so that it has become one with it. Now there seems to be no escape; we are it. Our past has become our present. The past millennia have become the new millennium. The animal has not evolved into human being — it has simply taken a human form and is pretending to be a human being.

Enlightened sage of modern times, J. Krishnamurti has gone deeper to say: "Violence takes many forms, not merely brutal action, striking each other. Violence includes imitation, conformity, obedience; it exists when you pretend to be which you are not. Aggression takes many forms — the polite, gentle aggressiveness, with a kid glove, persuading you through affection, compelling you to think along a particular line, that is violence. Non-violence is a non-fact; not a reality. It is a projection of thought in order to escape from or to accept violence and pretend that we are becoming non-violent. So, can we look at violence free from all that, free from escape, free from ideals, from suppression, and actually observe what violence is? When your mind is crippled by authority, as it is, it is very difficult to be free and so be able to look at violence."

The freedom from the brutal and violent past is only possible when we go through a deep cleansing of our unconsciousness. Meditation can bring about this metamorphosis. Osho says, "The only thing that can prevent a world war is that you start a totally new consciousness, that you start a new kind of humanity... a man who is capable of love, a man who is capable of meditation. Let love and meditation spread far and wide."

Let meditation reach to as many people as possible.

Image of God

Some people believe God created man in his own image. I sincerely doubt it. As I look around and witness the life and behaviour of most people, I have come to understand that man creates God in his own image. There are as many gods as there are men, and every man creates, believes and worships his own God. This is particularly true about the priests of the religions who are always busy creating all kind of images of gods for their gullible followers.

There are interesting stories of God's wrath in the holy scriptures. Jesus teaches love but one can find God's anger in many places in the Bible too. The expulsion of Adam and Eve from the Garden of Eden is the first example. Later in the book of *Genesis*, the nations gathered to build a tower that would reach the heavens, only to be destroyed by God and the people scattered. Another example comes in the book *Exodus* where the people fashioned a golden calf to worship when they got tired of waiting for Moses to descend from the mountain with the Ten Commandments.

There are other religions also with the same kind of unkind God who declares in their holy book: "I am not your uncle, I am not nice, I am jealous, I am angry." So this God is going to destroy those who don't understand this true nature of his.

This is a very strange statement! I thought uncles were basically nice and loving people.

All these statements project a certain image of God that is basically created by priests and their followers. Buddha rejected all this, as it was not based on reason and rationality. Untested beliefs lead to unlimited arguments and fights, death and destruction, which we see today. Buddha advises: "Do not believe anything on the mere authority of teachers or priests. Accept as true and as the guide to your life only that which accords with your own reason and experience, after thorough investigation. Accept only that which contributes to the well-being of yourself and others."

Osho admired the Buddha for what he was and what he taught. He said, "Buddha seems to be far more evolved even though he is not a God; he is only a human being. But he seems to be far more evolved because he has no anger; he is far more evolved because he has no jealousy. And certainly he is nice. Of course, he is far better than any uncle."

A new kind of approach is needed if we want peace in the world. That approach is of meditation and not of belief. All the ideologies about God will have to give way to meditation that is based on experiment and experience. It will be a way of scientific religiousness that will have nothing to do with any belief and fights about beliefs. It will be bliss of finding truth oneself and sharing it with others and inspiring others to find the same themselves. This is what enlightened people like the Buddha do. They don't believe or lead any crusades or *jihads* against others. They become examples of illumination themselves and their illumination shows the way of compassion and reverence for all life. Rage and revenge has no place in their religiousness.

IMAGE OF GOD

In Tune with Environment

You must have heard that Saint Francis used to talk to trees. He would say to an almond tree, "Sister, sing to me of God!" He would go to the river and talk to it and to fishes that were in the flowing waters. Nothing in existence was a stranger to him. The trees, the fish and the river do not understand our language, but they did understand what Saint Francis spoke to them. The language of love can be understood in silence by the inanimate objects. Even these come to life with the touch of love.

Man has forgotten to relate or communicate genially to his fellow-men. Then how will he communicate with trees and rocks, the fishes and the rivers, the whole nature in all its splendour? The whole idea of ecology depends on man's ability to communicate with nature. For long, all his training and education has taught him to dominate, exploit and destroy nature. Communication with nature has not been his education.

Here meditation plays a vital role. As a first step, meditation creates a space in which man learns to relate with himself, with his own inner nature. Remember, I am talking about relating with and not conquering and controlling the inner nature. One can relate only in friendliness.

OSHO FRAGRANCE

Then comes the next step of relating with nature outside — the trees, the mountains, the rivers and the whole cosmos. The outer ecology ultimately depends on the inner ecology of the man. If a man is loving and sensitive, his love and sensitivity will radiate to the trees, animals, birds, fellow human beings and the whole earth. His inner level of growth will determine his relationship with the outside world.

Meditation essentially changes the inner climate of man, brings harmony to his being, and creates a balance in his inner ecology. Once we become friendly with our own being, we become sensitive and compassionate with others too. A natural reverence flows through all our relations.

Talking on Khalil Gibran's *Messiah*, Osho says, "I will say religion is reverence for life. And if you don't have reverence for life, you cannot conceive the whole of existence — the trees and the birds and the animals — as different expressions of the same energy. In the source we are brothers and sisters with the animals and the birds and the trees; and if you start feeling this brotherhood, this sisterhood, you will find the first taste of what religion is."

It would be a good step to first take care of this inner environment so that the same positive energy in turn flows outward to the outer ecology. The outer ecology is being destroyed because the inner nature has been destroyed. It is just an outcome.

Osho says, "When a man is no more whole inside — he is divided, in conflict, like a fighting mob, in a crowd — that man creates disturbance in nature also. And these are related. When nature is destroyed and the natural systems are destroyed, then man has to face the consequences. Then again nature goes on affecting man and man goes on affecting nature. It is a vicious circle. But as I see it, the basic problem is somewhere inside man. If you are relaxed inside, if you have come to a settlement with your own nature, then you will be able to understand the natural functioning of the world, and you will not create any problem. You will not create any gap in it. You will see that everything is interconnected."

This reminds me of Saint Francis, because it was due to enlightened souls like him that we have examples for us on how to create harmony with nature and how to live a life full of love, since love is the greatest meditation possible.

To connect with the heart of the whole cosmos we need to have a harmonious heart. A heart that can sing. A heart that can dance. A heart that can throb with the whole cosmos.

Inner Peace

Apart from being Oxford of the East, Pune in western India is also famous among the people who want to discover inner pace. This city has a famous meditation resort, yoga centres and attracts people from all over the world who come here to seek peace and bliss.

A friend from Pune has written to me that she found another secret of inner peace. She writes: "I am passing this on to you because it definitely worked for me. By following the simple advice I read in an article, I have finally found inner peace. It said: 'The way to achieve inner peace is to finish all the things you've started.' So, yesterday I finished one bottle of vodka, a bottle of red wine, a bottle of Jack Daniels, all my Prozacs and a large box of chocolates. I feel better already!"

She tells me to pass this on to all those in need of inner peace. This lifestyle of living on a perpetual high with the help of stimulants, drugs and alcohol might be true for most people who cannot attain inner peace without indulging in heavy drinking and unhealthy eating in late hours. This is their daily routine and a must for good sleep. It makes them forget the problems of the world and also their own personal relationships.

I don't want to judge or condemn them. They have every right to live this way if they wish so long as they do not hurt others with their lifestyle of inner peace or as long as their inner peace does not become outer tension for others.

Somebody wrote to Osho: "Research over the past few years has suggested that certain states of consciousness brought about by meditation techniques appear to evoke specific brain-wave patterns. These states are now being created by electronic and auditory stimulation of the brain, and they can be learned through biofeedback. The traditional 'meditative state' — sitting silently (or at least quietly alert) is composed of bilateral, synchronous alpha waves. Deeper meditation also has bilateral theta waves. A state called 'lucid awareness' has the bilateral synchronous alpha and theta waves of deep meditation, plus the beta waves of normal thought processes. 'Lucid awareness' can be learned through biofeedback, using the most modern equipment. Are these kinds of stimulation and biofeedback useful tools for the meditator? What is the relationship of these technological techniques to the meditation beyond technique? Is this an example of bringing science together with meditation? I would like to experiment with these new technologies — both personally in my own meditation, and professionally in my work as a physician. Do I have your blessings?"

Osho replys: "It is perfectly good, you can study them. But remember that there is no shortcut to meditation, and no mechanical device can be of any help. In fact, meditation needs no technique — scientific or otherwise. Meditation is simply an understanding. It is not a question of sitting silently, it is not a question of chanting a *mantra*. It is a question of understanding the subtle workings of the mind. As you understand these workings of the mind, a great awareness arises in you which is not of the mind. That awareness arises in your being, in your soul, in your consciousness.

"Mind is only a mechanism, but when that awareness arises it is bound to create a certain energy pattern around it. That energy pattern is noted by the mind. Mind is a very subtle mechanism. And you are studying from the outside, so at the most you can study the mind. Seeing that whenever a person is silent, serene, peaceful, a certain wave pattern always inevitably appears in the mind; the scientific thinking will say: We can create this wave pattern in the mind, through some biofeedback technology, then the being inside will reach the heights of awareness. This is not going to happen. It is not a question of cause and effect."

Osho adds: "And you may go on practising with those scientific instruments for years; it will not change your character, it will not change your morality, it will not change your individuality. You will remain the same. Meditation transforms. It takes you to higher levels of consciousness and changes your whole lifestyle. It changes your reactions into responses to such an extent that it is unbelievable that the person who would have reacted in the same situation in anger is now acting in deep compassion, with love — in the same situation.

"Meditation is a state of being, arrived at through understanding. It needs intelligence; it does not need techniques. There is no technique that can give you intelligence. Otherwise, we would have changed all the idiots into geniuses; all the mediocre people would have become Albert Einsteins, Bertrand Russells, Jean-Paul Sartres. There is no way to change your intelligence from the outside, to sharpen it, to make it more penetrating, to give it more insight. It is simply a question of understanding, and nobody else can do it for you —no machine, no man."

Osho warns that for centuries the so-called gurus have been cheating humanity. Now, in the future, instead of gurus, these guru machines will cheat humanity. He said "A man who knows what meditation is cannot be deceived by any technique, because no technique can give you understanding of the working of the mind.

"For example, you feel anger, you feel jealousy, you feel hatred, you feel lust. Is there any technique that can help you to get rid of anger? Of jealousy? Of hatred? Of sexual lust? And if these things continue to remain, your lifestyle is going to remain the same as before.

"There is only one way — there has never been a second. There is one and only one way to understand that to be angry is to be stupid: Watch anger in all its phases, be alert to it so it does not catch you unawares; remain watchful, seeing every step of the anger. And you will be surprised, that as awareness about the ways of anger grows, the anger starts evaporating. And when the anger disappears, then there is a peace. Peace is not a positive achievement. When the hatred disappears, there is love. Love is not a positive achievement. When jealousy disappears, there is a deep friendliness towards all."

This is the real meditation, the true understanding, which can lead to inner peace.

Love, Meditate and Be Free

Osho is being read and heard like never before. There are about two thousand books based on his transcribed discourses in 90 languages, about one thousand hours of discourses on audio, and three thousand hours of videotapes.

But if his whole message were to be put in one word, I would say without hesitation that it is 'meditation'. If you want to add another word, it would be 'love'. And if you still insist for more, I will add 'celebration' and stop there.

Meditation is the foundation of Osho's vision. Love follows. Love without meditation is nothing more than lust. Meditation purifies it and makes it free from jealousy, possessiveness, and the bondage of expectation that ordinarily comes with the package of love. Freedom is a higher value than love; it is the very soul of love. When there is only meditation and no love, life becomes bland.

Osho says: "In my philosophy of life, only two things are valuable: One is meditation, the other is love. And both are complementary. Meditation means the joy of being alone, and love means the joy of being together with somebody."

"These are the two wings of a true education. Meditation

means independence, freedom — freedom from all, even from the beloved, because even the presence of the beloved encroaches on your space. It is good for the time being, it is good to overlap your space with somebody, it is good to meet and merge, but ultimately, and fundamentally, you are alone. And you have to learn how to be alone; and not only how to be alone, but joyously alone, ecstatically alone."

When you are in love, don't forget meditation. Love is not going to solve anything. Love is only going to show you who you are, where you are. And it is good that love makes you alert — alert of the whole confusion and the chaos within you. Now is the time to meditate! If love and meditation go together, you will have both the wings; you will have a balance.

A bird cannot fly with only one wing. A worldly man tries to fly only with one wing of love and falls flat on the ground. A *sannyasi* tries to fly with one wing of meditation and he cannot go very high; he falls back. A man of understanding, a balanced man, who can use both the wings can reach the Himalayan peaks of consciousness. And that point is the real celebration. We may call it bliss, *anandam*!

In short, this is Osho's legacy for all of us, for today and for the future. This is what he had been saying in thousands of ways while talking of all the ancient enlightened masters and mystics — Ashtavakra, Buddha, Jesus, Krishna, Gorakh, Kabir, Meera, Nanak, Patanjali, Lao Tsu, Heraclitus, Pythagoras, George Gurdjieff, Hasid, Sufi, Tantra and Zen masters, Zarathusthra... the list is simply endless.

Many people think that Osho is against the mystics. Somebody once asks him: "Are you against all other gurus?"

Osho replies: "Then who has been speaking on Lao Tzu and Chuang Tzu and Lieh Tzu, Bahaudin, Rabiya, Sanai, Bodhidharma, Rinzai, Bokuju, Milarepa, Marpa, Tilopa, Saraha, Kabir, Nanak, Meera, Jesus, Moses, Buddha, Mahavira? Who has been speaking about all these gurus, if I am against all gurus? But certainly I am against a few gurus — not because they are gurus, but because they are not gurus; they are pretenders. And I have not only spoken about ancient masters, I have spoken on Ramakrishna, Raman, Gurdjieff, Krishnamurti — I have spoken on contemporary masters too."

These masters are like flowers in God's garden who have the same fragrance. Osho invites all of humanity to enter this garden and relish this fragrance. There's no need to fight about which Master is better than the other; it is really stupid, because the people who keep fighting remain outside the garden. There's so much noise outside the garden — with the believers fighting and killing each other about the claims of superiority of their religion and belief system. These people have certainly no experience of the fragrance of religiousness. Osho says: "I teach religiousness and not religion."

Look Inward to Attain Enlightenment

We carry within us an infinite treasure of spiritual wealth. There is a vast kingdom of godliness within us — immeasurable and infinite. In order to open this window of godliness, we need a particular password, and that password is meditation.

We are living in the age of computers and robots. Working constantly with these mechanical gadgets, we end up behaving mechanically. And to behave like robots is not human because we do not remain masters of our life. Some other forces of unconsciousness control our life. There is no human glory or grace in this kind of existence. Osho reminds us: "Bring a little more awareness to your existence. Each act has to be done less automatically than you have been doing up to now, and you have the key. If you are walking, don't walk like a robot. Don't go on walking as you have always walked; don't do it mechanically. Bring a little awareness to it, slow down; let each step be taken in full consciousness."

Lord Buddha used to say to his disciples that when you raise your left foot, deep down say, 'left'. When you raise your right foot, deep down say, 'right'. First say it so that you can become acquainted with this new process. Then slowly let the words disappear; just remember, "Left, right, left, right."

Osho recommends, "Try it in small acts. You are not supposed to do big things. Eating, taking a bath, swimming, walking, talking, listening, cooking your food, washing your clothes — de-automatise the processes. Remember the word — de-automatisation, that is the whole secret of becoming aware. The mind is a robot. The robot has its utility; this is the way the mind functions. You learn something; when you learn it in the beginning you are aware. For example, if you learn to drive a car you are very alert. After all, it is so dangerous, that's why you have to be aware. But the moment you have learnt driving, this awareness will not be needed. Then the robotic part of your mind will take over." And this is when we lose our consciousness. Meditation simply means regaining our consciousness and transcending our mind that functions like a robot. And this transcendence happens within the realm of our inner being, our consciousness.

143

According to Osho, "The mind opens outside; meditation opens inside."

The mind is a door that leads outside in the world; meditation is the door that leads to your interiority – to the very innermost shrine of your being. And suddenly, you are enlightened.

Timeless Mysteries of the Universe

This universe is a mysterious phenomenon. Mysterious because it is alive and to understand the mysteries, one has to be either a mystic or a scientist. The Hindus have always believed that *kan kan mein Bhagwan*. (It essentially means that God resides in each particle of dust).

Other mystics, too, have also said that we are always walking on the holy ground. To a spiritual person, everything is divine; God exists in every aspect of life. But to a non-spiritual person, everything is mundane and meaningless. A spiritual person feels a strong energy around him all the time. Even the universe keeps showering life-energy on him all the time because he becomes receptive. Only receptive people can feel the energy and hence remain in high spirits. They're filled with reverence towards all the forms of life around them. They walk, talk and relate differently because they are interacting with various forms and levels of godliness. They will not be abusive to anybody because deep within their hearts they know that this alive universe is recording each word they utter and their words will keep resonating endlessly, so why fill this universe with nonsense?

Scientists say that the words and sounds don't die. With

certain fine instruments we can catch those sounds that were uttered thousands of year ago. Maybe some day one can record the magical words spoken by the Buddha, Lord Krishna, Meera Bai, Kabir and Guru Nanak.

A meditator will not need any such instruments as he will be able to listen to such messages directly in his meditation. It will be through his inner tuning. That's what happened to Prophet Mohammed when the process of *ilham* took place in his meditation. Meera listened to the flute of Krishna after thousands of years. The message of the enlightened mystics does not depend on the printed books only — it descends in the heart of their real devotees and remains there.

Osho says, "My own experience is that wherever anybody has become enlightened, there are certain vibrations still. Thousands of years may have passed but those vibrations are still there — in the trees, earth and mountains. You can still feel some strange kind of presence. The man is not there, the singer may have died, but his record is still there and you can hear the voice again."

A Garland of Miracles

A friend once asked me about my beliefs. I said that I do not believe in anything except miracles. Every moment millions of miracles are happening all around — I wonder why we cannot see them. I exist, and it is a miracle. You exist and that is a miracle. We all exist, which is also a miracle. Life is a garland of miracles.

One moment life appears in various colours, shapes and sizes, and seems to be very solid, as if it is something permanent. Next moment it disappears or evaporates as if it never existed. Isn't this a miracle? And the same life appears again out of nowhere in all its freshness. Our minds may become stuck and attached with only certain forms of life as we tend to seek safety and security in our relationships. And when those certain forms to which we cling, disappear, we start feeling miserable. Our minds want to believe that those relationships were permanent. But life has no obligations to function according to our expectations.

Meditation gives us eyes to see this reality with clarity. We should start rejoicing in life as it comes and goes. There is a life and there is a death every moment. Moment to moment life moves into death and the death into life. It is an ongoing inter-play of life and **death**. **This** is the only miracle worth calling a miracle; all other miracles pale into insignificance. This is *Prabhu leela*, God's playfulness, which is always exciting, and never boring. But isn't it a miracle that we often feel bored?

In his discourse, *Ah, This*, Osho says: "You have made life boring — some achievement! Life is such a dance of ecstasy and you have reduced it to boredom. You have done a miracle! What else do you want to do? You can't do anything bigger than this. Life and boring? You must have a tremendous capacity to ignore life."

He explains: "Life is not boring, but the mind is boring. And we create such a mind, such a strong mind, like a China Wall around ourselves, that it does not allow life to enter into us. It disconnects us from life. We become isolated, encapsulated, windowless. Living behind a prison wall you don't see the morning sun, you don't see birds on the wing, you don't see the sky in the night full of stars. And you start thinking that life is boring. Your conclusion is wrong."

A really meditative person embraces life each moment with such freshness that he does not feel any boredom. Miracles greet him all the time as he is receptive to them.

147

Slim Meditation

"My methods of meditation are ways that will make you expand your energy. Energy is like seeds. One seed can make a whole earth green. One small sparkle or energy in you can fill the whole earth with dance, song, music. Just a little sparkle is enough. If you know how to expand it, it can become a wild fire. It may be just a little flame within you. Meditation is nothing but an effort to expand your inner flame so that you can become afire, aflame, aglow, overflowing." says Osho.

Long-term stress could make people fat — claims a study of around 50 overweight middle-aged Swedish men, published last week. Disruptions in the human nervous system or stress can concentrate fat around the abdomen, raising risk of diabetes and heart problems — a study by the university hospital in the Swedish city of Gothenburg found.

The eastern yoga and meditation system offers a perfect solution to this problem. If yoga is too arduous for people, there is Osho's *Kundalini* meditation. We recommend this method to be practised daily for 21 days for marvellous results. It has been effective at Osho centres worldwide. In 1998, a special survey revealed people all over the world, specially USA, were suffering from Internet depression. News agency AFP distributed the story about *Kundalini* meditation as a cure for Net blues. The report said, "A body under stress creates a surplus of one hormone which stimulates a fat-gathering enzyme. This enzyme is more easily taken up by the abdomen than other parts of the body. After a long period of stress, hormone surplus decreases but fat remains, particularly around the bellies of modern men who need less physical exercise to survive than their forefathers."

Yoga has its own research. People who live an emotionally suppressed and unsatisfied life eat more, accumulating stress and fat in their body. This can be cured with cathartic techniques such as Osho Dynamic Meditation. The first step is vigorous breathing for 10 minutes. The second step is of catharsis for 10 minutes. The third step is of hammering on coiled energy of *kundalini* below the *muladhaar chakra*. Then, there are two steps of 15 minutes of silence and celebration. This is a powerful meditation to tone the body. Osho's *Kundalini* meditation lasts for an hour and has four stages of which three are with music composed under the guidance of Osho. If you would like to try, it is described below. Remember the last stage is in silence. A gong signals the end of the silent period.

First stage: 15 minutes

Loosen up and let your body shake, feeling energies moving up your feet. Let go everywhere and become the shaking. Keep eyes open or closed.

Second stage: 15 minutes

Dance any way you feel. Let the body move anyway.

Third stage: 15 minutes

Close your eyes and be still, sitting or standing. Witness what happens inside and out.

Fourth stage: 15 minutes

Keep your eyes closed, lie down and be still.

"...Allow the shaking, don't do it. Stand silently and feel it coming. When your body starts to tremble, help it, don't do it. If you force it, it will become an exercise. Then shaking will be there but just on the surface. You will remain solid, stone like, rock like within; you will remain a manipulator, the doer, and the body will just follow. The body is not the question — you are the question."

Turn on, Tune in and Drop the Lot

Meditation is a celebration of one's being for there's nothing lacking in existence. But we are preoccupied with becoming 'something' or 'somebody' — and we think that we will be happy and satisfied only when we have reached 'somewhere'.

The art of meditation is the 'here-now' principle. Its flowering is celebration. Zen philosophy says: "Turn on, tune in and drop the lot." Turn on means become fully alive in the moment. Tune in means look within and get connected with your inner being. And drop the lot means drop all that garbage you collect in your mind. Reality is 'here-now'. Be in the 'eternal now' and celebrate the purity of your being — that which is, that what you are in your authenticity.

Osho says: "Celebration means dropping this whole trip of becoming and just being here. When becoming disappears, all the smoke of becoming disappears; there is the flame of being. And that very flame is celebration. To celebrate is as natural as it is for the trees to bloom, for birds to sing, for rivers to flow to the ocean; it is a natural state. It has nothing to do with your desires, hopes and their fulfillment. But to see the celebration that is already happening at the deepest core of your being you will have to drop becoming."

It is futile to seek God outside of us. Life and God are not separate. Every pebble, every leaf, every drop of water, is full of God. When you are thirsty, God is thirsty within you. And when you drink cold water, it is God flowing within your being; it is God who will quench your thirst. The thirst is God, the quenching is God, the water that quenches is God. All is God. So what will you renounce? For what reason should you fast?

Osho says: "You are not to achieve something; it has already been given to you. It is God's gift. You are already where you should be; you can't be anywhere else. There is nowhere to go, nothing to achieve. So you can celebrate. Then there is no hurry, worry, anxiety, anguish, or fear of being a failure. It is impossible to fail, because there is no question of success. It is just a conditioning by the society that creates the problem in you. You start thinking, 'I am not reaching anywhere, and life is slipping out of my hands and death is coming closer. Am I going to make it or not?' And then there is the great fear of missing, of frustration that so much is lost. 'I have not yet been able to prove myself, my worth'."

One who has understood that the journey of becoming leads nowhere except to mirages and misery, starts feeling content in his own being. As the understanding grows, the contentment grows and ripens into real happiness and bliss. One starts enjoying everything that this life offers.

In *The Art of Dying*, Osho says: "Don't wait for some great bliss to descend on you. It never happens. Great bliss is nothing but small pleasures accumulating in your being. The total of all the small pleasures is the great bliss. Eating, enjoy it. Drinking, enjoy it. Taking a bath, enjoy it. Walking, enjoy it."

In the *Heart Sutra*, Osho says: "In your very body, in your very being, this very moment, God is there — and you have not celebrated it. You cannot celebrate. Celebration has to happen first in your own home, at close quarters. Then it becomes a great tidal wave."

You are in love — celebrate while it is there! Don't start making arrangements so that it is always there; otherwise, you will miss the moment in making arrangements. And by the time arrangements are ready, the flower is dead. By the time you are ready to enjoy, the moment has already gone. And nobody can bring it back, there is no going back. The river is onward and onward flowing, and you are being thrown to new shores every moment.

Silvery Magic of the Full Moon

A full-moon night is the best time for meditation, when the noises of the day give way to the silence of the night. Open your heart and let your eyes be filled with the moon's nectar. Absorb this nectar into your whole being. Feel the coolness and the tenderness in the atmosphere.

Let this atmosphere be metamorphosed into an *atma*-sphere, the soul space. Let your body sway or dance gently, and bring yourself into the realm of grace. The more you can melt the more you can move upward into the vast sky of consciousness.

We carry within us both the mountains and valleys. We can get high and feel on top of the world, reaching the Everest of our consciousness. We could also feel down in the dumps as if we are in a black hole. Human consciousness can throw us into the dark dismal ditches, or it can help us open our wings, soaring high into the sky.

Consciousness is a liquid phenomenon, so is moon-energy. Its powerful presence in the sky resonates in our inner sky of consciousness. It affects our psyche.

In his discourse 'Celebrate Myself: God is Nowhere, Life is Now Here', Osho says: "The full moon night has a specialness that is now being recognised by science."

But scientists approach it from the wrong side, because they are living on the wrong side of the earth, in the West. They became aware that more murders are committed on full moon nights, more suicides happen, more people go insane... The full moon night affects the ocean — waves become very tidal — as if the ocean is trying to reach out to the moon.

Man consists of 80 per cent water, so something in him also starts feeling a subtle vibration. Scientists say man is the other end of the evolutionary progress — in the beginning it was the fish. So we have a deep connection.

Osho says: "We are carrying great potential of which we are utterly unaware. It is painful to break that hard shell (of ignorance), but once you are ready to go through the pain, and once the shell is broken, life takes a quantum leap. You become immortal. You are no more darkness; you become a full-moon night. And you know misery no more. Bliss simply becomes your nature, your very existence.

155

"The moon represents the most blissful and beautiful phenomenon. One can become that beauty, that splendour. It is within our reach. For we can hold the moon in our hearts. Going to the moon is useless. Far more significant is the process of bringing the moon in.

"The moon creates magic every night. It simply reflects the sun's rays, functioning only as a mirror. The Master, too, is a mirror, and meditation makes you a mirror — clean and pure, so everything is reflected in you as it is, devoid of judgment."

The moon, just by reflecting them, transforms the hot rays of the sun into cool energy. As a Master, he absorbs the same energy that you absorb, he eats the same food as you eat, he drinks the same water, he breathes the same air, but some alchemical change is constantly going on in him.

On the full-moon night of every month, Zen practitioners watch the moon all night. And as they go on witnessing the moon, a deep tranquillity and silence descends over them, particularly on the night when Gautam Buddha was born, became enlightened, and died. So this is a special night for Zen Buddhists.

A Laboratory for Human Transformation

Most people who are progressing on a spiritual path are aware of the unique Russian mystic, G.I. Gurdjieff. He had a meditation centre, a sort of commune, on the outskirts of Paris. Many mystics have tried to create communes, as in ancient times, our sages used to have *ashrams*. A commune or *ashram* functions as a human laboratory for the transformation of an individual, a seeker of truth. Gurdjieff also had such a commune, in which a Russian man, Anton also lived. He was older and not much liked by the other members, because his lifestyle was a bit clumsy and irritating to others. The other members of the commune started treating him as an outcast.

Once Gurdjieff went abroad. In his absence, Anton decided to leave the commune with the intention of never returning again. His fellow commune members celebrated his departure as good riddance. Gurdjieff returned and was unhappy to know that Anton had left. He inquired from the members about where to find Anton and went to the city to look for him. After riding around for a while in the streets of Paris, he found him sitting somewhere.

Gurdjieff invited Anton to come and live in the commune once again. Anton refused even though he had no place to stay.

The other members living in the commune were paying for their stay while Anton did not have any money to pay. But for a Master or a mystic like Gurdjieff, money was not the criterion. Mystics don't look at life this way and their attitude is not utilitarian. For them the individual is more important than money.

Gurdjieff looked into the eyes of Anton with compassion and invited him to come back and live in the commune for free. He had magnetic eyes with a piercing look. Anton could not say no to the Master. When the other commune members saw Anton coming back with the Master, they could not hide their dislike for him. They felt jealous that they had to pay for their stay while this dirty man was getting everything free. But Gurdjieff was a stubborn Master who told the members not to judge Anton this way, but look at him as a mirror. A human being can function as a mirror to other human beings — to see their own faces. They can see their beauty or ugliness, jealousy or generosity, cruelty or compassion, love or hate. Anton was very valuable this way.

This exactly is the role of the commune or the purpose of living together in a commune, as the latter becomes a place of real transformation. The same is possible in our work situations and we can really benefit from all our relationships if we let them function as mirrors. We can examine ourselves and grow to be responsible human beings. Osho talks about responsibility, which really means the ability to respond.

Meditation is the Key

While on the way to Shimla we were going to participate in a meditation camp, I asked a new friend, a fellow-traveller, "Do you also meditate?"

He said, "I meditate in my own way." Yes, one can really meditate in one's own way — and there are as many ways to meditate, as there are people in the world.

Existence expresses itself every time in original ways. Every flower blooms in its own way, though all the flowers may look very much the same. Look at them carefully and you will notice the subtle difference — that subtle something makes all the difference. No real flower on earth is a carbon copy of another flower. Only the plastic flowers produced in a factory are identical. On a mountain you won't even find two stones that are similar, though the thousands of factory tiles produced out of stones are alike. Existence does not believe in duplicates or copies. Existence is so infinite that it can continue to produce original expressions till infinity. 'Original' simply means something that emerges out of the origin, the source. Existence celebrates originality.

There is a beautiful word in Hindi — *utsa*. It means 'the source'. And there is an other word — *utsav* — that means 'celebration'. Something that emerges from *utsa*, the source becomes *utsav*, the celebration! The real celebration is not possible with duplicates. It is possible only with something that is original. This whole existence is continuously celebrating, because everything manifests from the source.

Meditation simply means the realisation of this source, getting connected with the source. In our imagination, in our mind, we may think that we have gone too far away from the source. In reality, we are always connected with the source. Meditation means returning to the source. And millions of people on earth could return to their source — not in the imagination, but in reality, and each in his own way. That would be their unique method of meditation. What is important, is that one meditates — and not how one meditates! What is important is that one prays — and not how one prays! What is important is that one loves — and not how one loves! Attaining to inner richness of love, prayer and meditation is all that is significant. This ends the whole dispute and quarrel of spiritual methods and meaningless claims of wrong and right. What works for me might not work for you; what works for someone may not work for the other. And Buddha's famous statement is: 'Truth is what works.'

Osho says: "Buddha has defined truth as that which works. If a lie works, it is true. And if a truth cannot work, of what use is it? Throw it into the garbage can; it is of no use. Buddha's definition is really wonderful. He was the first pragmatist in the world. Now scientists agree with the Buddha — though science took 25 centuries to learn the secret!"

Tao Wisdom: Meditation is not Utilitarian

Meditation is attracting people in a big way these days. People often ask about the benefits of meditation. "What are we going to gain in meditation? Does meditation give us wealth and prosperity, besides peace of mind?"

The only answer to such questions is: "No. Meditation is not something mundane or utilitarian; it is not for business or for material gains. If you are hankering for material gains through meditation, you will become victims of those who sell all kinds of packages in the name of meditation. Sadly, large-scale businesses run by unenlightened people are flourishing all over the country. An enlightened person will never promise any material gains in this world or spiritual gains in the other world."

Meditation is transcendental. It can be done in the marketplace but it does not belong to the marketplace. Rather, it's a sharing of peace and bliss by those who have attained it.

There's an interesting Tao story told by Osho, which goes like this:

Lao Tzu was walking with his disciples and they came to a forest where hundreds of carpenters were cutting trees, because a great palace was being built. So, the whole forest had been almost cut, but only one tree was standing there, a big tree with thousands of branches. Lao Tzu asked his disciples to go and inquire why this tree had not been cut yet when the whole forest had been cut.

The disciples asked the carpenters, " Why have you not cut this tree?"

The carpenters said, "This tree is useless. You cannot make anything out of it because every branch has so many knots in it. Nothing is straight. You cannot make pillars or furniture out of it. You cannot use it as fuel because the smoke is dangerous to the eyes. This tree is absolutely useless, that's why."

They came back. Lao Tzu laughed and he said, "Be like this tree. If you want to survive in this world, be like this tree, absolutely useless. Then nobody will harm you. If you are straight you will be cut, you will become furniture in somebody's house. If you are beautiful, you will be sold in the market, you will become a commodity. Be like this tree, absolutely useless. Then nobody can harm you. And you will grow vast, and thousands of people can find shade under you."

A man of meditation becomes such a huge tree. Thousands of seekers of truth attain to meditation and benediction in his presence. Buddha, Mahavira, Krishna, Kabir, Nanak, Farid, Meera and so many enlightened mystics and sages were such trees whose eternal message and everlasting energy in the cosmos is helping humanity even today.

Meditate, and Feel Suffused with Love

Meditation is a way of living life full of love and consciousness. It is not about going to temples, praying hurriedly and yet continue living life mechanically and accidentally. Meditation means to bring awareness to each act — big and small.

The quality of love and acts of meditation go hand in hand. "If you meditate," says Osho, "you will be simply loving; it will be just a quality of your being. And then it has a different flavour and does not create a bondage. Then you share unconditionally and your love is just the way you are."

Osho tells an anecdote: Once a Hassidic mystic was travelling with his disciples. They came to a *serai*. In the morning, the keeper of the *serai* served tea and breakfast. While they were drinking their tea, suddenly, the keeper fell at the Master's feet, ecstatic — crying and laughing together.

His disciples were puzzled. How could he know that this man was the Master? It was supposed to be a secret and the disciples were told that nobody should be told who the Master is. The Master was travelling incognito. Who had told this *serai*-keeper? The disciples were worried. They inquired, but nobody had told; nobody had even talked to that man. The Master said: "Don't be puzzled. Ask this man himself, how he recognised me. Nobody has told him; he has still recognised."

So they asked: "We cannot recognise him. Even we are suspicious about whether he is truly enlightened or not, and we have lived with him for many years. Still, a suspicion somewhere goes on lurking. How have you recognised?"

The man replied: "I have been serving tea and breakfast and food to thousands of people, and I have never come across a man who has looked with such deep love at the teacup. I could not help but recognise. I know all sorts of people passing from here but I have never seen anybody looking at the teacup with such love, as if somebody is looking at one's beloved."

Osho explains that this man must have had a totally different quality; he must be full of love. Otherwise, who looked at a teacup with such love? A teacup is a teacup. You have to use it. It is a utility item. You don't look with love. In fact, you don't look at you own wife with love. She is a utility, a teacup to be used and thrown away. You don't look at your husband with love. The husband is a means. Love is possible only when everything becomes the end. Then even a teacup has the quality of the beloved.

Reverence for Life is Non-violence

What is God? The modern word for God is existence, as it was also understood in the time of Mahavira, the twenty-fourth Tirthankara of Jain religion.

He did not believe in God but he talked about existence. He said that it is existence which includes everything and takes care of everything.

Osho tells a beautiful story about the life of Mahavira. Once he was going from one village to another village with his close disciple, Goshalak. Mahavira told his disciple: "Your responsibility towards existence shows how much you have attained your authentic reality. We cannot see your authentic reality but we can see your responsibility."

As they were walking, they come across a small plant. Goshalak being a logician, pulled the plant and threw it away. It was a small plant with small roots. On seeing him do this, Mahavira said, "This is irresponsibility. But you cannot do anything against existence. You can try, but it is going to backfire."

So Goshalak said, "What can existence do to me? I have pulled this plant; now existence cannot bring it to life again."

Mahavira only laughed at this. Later they went into the town for food. On their return they were surprised to see that the plant was rooted again. While they were in the town, it had started raining, and the roots of the plant, finding the support of the rain, went back into the soil. They were small roots, it was windy, and the wind helped the plant to stand up again.

By the time they returned, the plant was back to its normal position.

Mahavira said, "Look at the plant. I told you that you cannot do anything against existence. You can try, but that will turn against you, because that will go on separating you from existence. It will not bring you closer.

"Just see that plant. Nobody could have imagined that this will happen. It is going to live its life. It seems to us a small plant but it is part of a vast universe, a vast existence, of the greatest power there is. From this point our paths separate. I cannot allow a man to live with me who is against existence and feels no responsibility."

Osho points out that Mahavira's whole philosophy of non-violence can be better expressed as the philosophy of reverence for existence. Non-violence is simply a part of it. The more you find yourself responsible for people, things, existence, the more you can be at ease that you are on the right track.

Shiva & Shakti

The power that comes out of meditation does not come as power. It comes as if flowers are showering on you; it comes as fragrance, it comes as love, it comes as compassion. It brings all the great qualities and all the great values of life suddenly to their blossoming. It is the spring of your consciousness. Everything suddenly becomes green, everything becomes cool; the breeze becomes full of fragrance, because you are bursting forth into flowers which cannot be seen by the eye. But those who have the heart and the courage to open to it will certainly feel it. They will feel its song, they will feel its dance.

—Osho

Future Belongs to Feminine Qualities

I gnorance shuts the iron gates but love opens them.

The sound of the gates opening wakes the beautiful woman asleep. Kabir says, *"Don't let a chance like this go by."*

Explaining this poem of mystic Kabir, Osho says: "The sound of the gates opening wakes the beautiful woman who is asleep.

"Now these are symbolic words. According to Kabir, your soul is the sleeping woman. He is using the word woman for your soul, your consciousness, because only the feminine qualities are authentically spiritual qualities. Beauty is feminine, honesty is feminine, sincerity is feminine; all that is great within your consciousness is feminine. Even the word consciousness is feminine. In English it is difficult, because in English you don't make a difference in words, you don't make a difference between male and female in each word. But in any language that is born in the East, each word has the distinction: consciousness, awareness, *samadhi, sambodhi*, all are feminine.

"And the man of love and compassion starts having a feminine beauty and a feminine grace. The male is a little barbarous. His qualities are that of a warrior, fighter, egoist, chauvinist, fanatic, fascist. The male qualities are qualities of a Nazi. It is not strange that Germany is the only country which calls its own land, the fatherland. The whole world calls their countries the mother land — Germany is a special case. It is time they should change it; they should stop calling it the fatherland because that gives male qualities the priority."

It is really true that the too much appreciation of the male qualities has been the real cause of most of the wars in the world. Almost all the wars have been fought by men. Women had little participation in wars. The world is always busy in wars because we have been appreciating male qualities and condemning feminine qualities in people. Somebody who is disinterested in fighting is labelled as effeminate. And if a boy starts weeping, we ask him: "Why are you crying like women? Be a man!" This philosophy of condemning feminine qualities is the root cause of all wars in the world and it provokes aggressiveness and barbarianism in men.

We want our male children to become brave heroes or at least imbibe some of the qualities of great men. This appreciation of aggressive male qualities has been more dominant in the West.

German philosopher, Friedrich Nietzsche condemned Gautam Buddha because of his feminine grace and beauty. He looked very feminine to Nietzsche, because his idea of a real man was to be strong and be made of steel. Buddha was the most compassionate and cultured man, the most graceful man this world has ever known. But his compassion, grace and beauty are essentially feminine qualities that have been adored and worshipped in the East. Nietzsche condemned Gautam Buddha's teachings also. He said that he could not appreciate his teachings as they were harmful to humanity. He warned that if people believed in the Buddha's teachings, the whole world would turn into a feminine world. Nietzsche appreciated the warrior, the military man, who is always ready to kill or be killed. The sound of military parade, the rhythmic noise of marching the armed forces to the war zone was real music to his ears.

This philosophy gives birth to Hitler. If we follow his philosophy we will have more world wars and no peace. If we want peace in the world, we will have to nurture feminine qualities to create a balance in the world. Osho says: "It is true that all great qualities are feminine — love, compassion, sympathy, kindness. All these qualities have a flavour of the feminine. We have been giving too much emphasis to the head and ignoring the heart. We are living an utterly miserable life because we have got hung up in our heads and have bypassed our hearts. The head has dried our poetry of emotions, the sentiments, the smiles, the tears, the laughter and made our life so boring. Friendship has disappeared from the world because our head calculates too much. The head is miserly and calculative. This is the head that has created such monstrous concrete jungles and man has no time to look into the sky and dance with the clouds and rejoice in the rains. The heart wants to sing and the head thinks about society and worries about what others will say about us. The head has made us too serious in the name of sanity. We need some amount of feminine insanity of love and emotions to bring some balance to our miserable life.

"This feminine madness is far better than Nietzsche's male madness. Give women a chance and non-violence will effortlessly be the religion of the new millennium. The new millennium should have a totally new vision and values of life, in which women give their significant contribution of feminine qualities to men, use their feminine power for peace. Let the head and heart unite in meditation and create a new BEING in the world."

Osho Fragrance

Says Osho in A *Sudden Clash of Thunder*: "God is more of a mother than a father. God is more like a womb than anything else. Out of God we are born, and back into God we dissolve. He is our birth and He is our death. He is like the ocean: He 'waves' us, we become His waves; He absorbs us — we disappear. He is compassion, He is love. All His qualities are feminine."

Venus in the Sky with Diamonds

We are fortunate that beautiful things are happening in our lifetime — as no one alive today could have been witness to such a spectacular event on June 8 when the rarest solar eclipse by Venus was visible to 75 per cent of Earth. Last time this transit happened in 1882.

What does this mean for humans? It is like a momentary (in the universe the time-scale is not the same, a moment could be not less than eternity) Nataraj dance of Shiva and Shakti. The Sun is Lord Shiva or the male and Venus, our Goddess Parvati or the Shakti — and it is their celestial interplay. Shakti, the Venus, is all powerful to eclipse Shiva, the sun. Astrologically speaking, it does have significance in people's love life. Frank McNally, an Irish astrologer says, "There's bad news and good news about Venus's transit across the face of the sun. If you look at it directly, it could seriously damage eyesight. But it could improve love life."

This universe is an organic phenomenon — there's inner connectivity. The smallest blade of grass on Earth is connected with the farthest, unseen star. We are affected in positive or negative ways by these beings. It is natural because we get affected even by meaningless things. A dog passing by, a cat walking around us trigger something in us. We live in the world of vibrations.

In existence, everything is constantly vibrating — and we are vibrating with everything. This is the heart beat of the universe. The harmony of opposites like *yin* and *yang*, day and night, Shiva and Shakti, male and female. Their longing to meet and merge when they become separated.

In reality they are never separated — they only appear to be. Transits of Venus are rare and powerful. Women are from Venus, we all know. So when the planet aligns with the sun, according to the website astrologycom.com, "The principal life force is united with love, female energy, harmony, and the goddess principle." A transit promises everything from romantic breakthroughs to "great shifts in human consciousness". And if we meditate in such moments we may become fully enlightened. This meeting of man and woman is not confined to the outside world — a deeper meeting happens inside, because deep down we are both.

173

Modern psychology, particularly the Jungian School of Psychology, is based on the premise that man is bisexual and so is woman. If your conscious mind is a man, your unconscious will be a woman.

But to manage the inner meeting is difficult first because it is invisible. First learn the lesson with the visible. Meet with outer woman, outer man. Then search in, find polarity. The day inner man and woman meet, you are enlightened.

Unless you know the woman outside, in richness, sweetness and bitterness, and the outer man in beauty and ugliness, you will not be able to move to the inner dimension. You will not be able to allow Shiva and Shakti to meet inside. And that meeting is of utter importance because only then do you become a God.

VENUS IN THE SKY WITH DIAMONDS

Krishna's Feminine Side

One cannot imagine Krishna without Radha. Some people believe that Radha was not a historical person. Whether she was a real person or not, is immaterial. What is important is the fact that the word *radha* is a metaphor.

Radha as a metaphor is very beautiful and unique. The word carries a deep meaning for the spiritual seekers and devotees. Radha is a reverse dimension of *dhara*, which means a rivulet that was born out of the ocean.

Search for God or for the truth is the search for our source — the origin!

Osho explains: "In Sanskrit, when the river moves towards the sea, from the origin to the goal, it is called *dhara*. If the river can move backwards, not towards the sea but towards the origin itself, then it is called *radha*. *Dhara* written backwards becomes *Radha*. *Radha* simply means one who has started searching for the origin, for the very source from where we are coming. And the only way to reach the source is to become a lover of existence."

Hindus worship Krishna as the perfect incarnation of God. He absorbs everything in himself — all the contradictions. He is the best lover who plays his flute and dances with thousands of *gopis* and then shares the highest wisdom of life in the battle- ground without getting disturbed. In short, he represents the whole existence. And Radha, his beloved, represents one who is in tremendous love with him and listening to his call, rushes back to him.

There cannot be any rivulet without the sea. There cannot be any Radha without Krishna. The sea can be there without the rivulets, and Krishna can be there without Radha. Yet, this perfect incarnation of God will not be considered totally perfect without Radha. We just cannot imagine the perfection without Radha. Radha does add something very significant to his perfection. He becomes more perfect if that can be said. Presence of Radha with Krishna creates an eternal romance, the *maharaas* of existence, the inter-play of man-woman love relationship.

Osho says: "Radha constitutes the whole of Krishna's tenderness and refinement; whatever is delicate and fine in him comes from Radha. She is his song, his dance and all that is feminine in him. Alone Krishna is an out and out male, and therefore, there is no meaning in mentioning his name alone. That is why they become united and one; they become Radha Krishna. Both the extremes of life meet and mingle in Radha Krishna. And this adds to Krishna's completeness."

175

Relationships

177

Walk in the marketplace like a Buddha. Live in the world... the world is very enriching, because relationship mirrors. All relationships are mirrorlike. You see your face in the mirror of the other's being. It is very difficult to see your own face directly — you will need the other, the mirror, to see your own face. And where can you find a better mirror than the eyes of the other?

—Osho

Relationship between Father and Son

Once I visited a *sannyasin* friend of mine named Swami Kapil. We were busy chatting when Kapil's father came in. I had never met his father earlier, so Kapil introduced me to him, saying: "Meet my 'biological father'." I felt embarrassed to hear a statement like that but I saw that Kapil was totally comfortable in introducing his father in this way. Visibly, his father also did not feel anything wrong with this statement; maybe he felt, but he chose not to show it.

This incidence is 20 years old but is still fresh in my memory, because it sounded very odd. Though it is a fact, but I felt that it showed a complete absence of respect for the father.

It is so difficult to show respect towards the father who has always dominated the son in his childhood — that's why the idea of celebrating a day in a year as Father's Day may have originated. This day has its origin in the guilt feelings dwelling deep in the sons. Poor father! He does so much for his children but what we often see is an endless conflict between them, especially between fathers and sons.

Osho talks about a great Russian novelist, Turgnev, who has written a book — perhaps his best, his masterpiece — *Fathers and Sons*. The book is about the struggle between the fathers and sons, because the fathers would like the sons to be their replicas. Naturally, they will not allow the sons any freedom. Obedience they expect and they expect their sons to be carbon copies of their own self.

He says in this book that the relationship between a father and son is always one of conflict. There is no other tie, except the tie of conflict between them. The son is the rightful successor of the father and therefore, is always engaged in removing him. He waits eagerly for him to vacate his position. The son hates the dominance of the father in most family affairs. When this becomes intolerable or unbearable for the son, he can even go to the extent of killing his father in anger.

If we look at this situation in psychological terms, we come across some startling revelations.

Freud did a lot of research on this subject. He says that people worship God as father because sometime in the beginning they must have killed some dominant father, somebody who was too dictatorial. It is a well-known fact that many a king have been killed by their sons because the king lived on, making the heir wait endlessly. The son on coming of age and seeing that he was not going to live to be a king, was left with the only possibility — death of the father. Many kings have imprisoned their fathers and taken over the throne, because they saw that there seemed to be no possibility of his natural death — at least while there was time to enjoy being a king! What would be the point of becoming the ruler when you are 75 or 80 when your father dies and you succeed? Within a year or two you would be gone too.

Osho appreciates the psychological insights of Sigmund Freud who says that because somewhere in the past man had to kill the father, he felt the guilt of what he had done. And out of that guilt he started worshipping the ancestors, the fathers, the elderly people, old people. All this respect has arisen out of a guilt that is deep set in the human heart. Man started inventing a God as father, raising temples in his memory, statues, priests praying, worshippers worshipping. Behind this whole scene and drama of religion, Sigmund Freud finds only one single fact and that is: Somewhere in the past man had behaved so badly with his father — perhaps murdered him — that he cannot forgive him. So the only way is to pray, make God your father, the Creator of the world. All these hypotheses... a very original insight.

Lao Tzu says: "The more you try to make sons listen to their fathers, the more they will go against their fathers."

And Lao Tzu has been proved correct. In the last five thousand years, man has tried to make the son obedient to the father and the result is an increasing abyss between the two. A son touches his father's feet and calculates what he will inherit from him. It is said that the sons of rich fathers never lament the father's death. They cannot; perhaps they are happy. The sons of kings have been known to bring about the death of their fathers. All around us there are manipulations and calculations.

There is no inner necessity that the son should agree with the father. In fact it seems far better that he should not agree. That's how evolution happens. If every child agrees with the father then there will be no evolution, because the father will agree with his own father, so everybody will be where God left Adam and Eve — naked, outside the gate of the Garden of Eden. Everybody will be there. Because sons have disagreed with their fathers, forefathers, with their whole tradition and thus, man has evolved.

This whole evolution is a tremendous disagreement with the past.

The inner journey of truth begins with the help of a Master who has already attained the truth.

The illumination of the Master becomes an invitation to the unlit lamp of the disciple who gropes in the dark, looking for somebody who can show him the way. To find such a Master is really a blessing, a benediction. Half of the inner journey is over by meeting such a Master and the other half is over when the disciple comes to fruition and becomes a Master himself.

Somebody asks Osho: "Who are you?"

Osho replies: "I am an invitation. I am an invitation for all those who are seeking, searching, and have a deep longing in their hearts to find their home."

A true enlightened Master is an open invitation to one and all, without any discrimination of caste, colour or creed. He invites everybody to come and drink from the river of his wisdom, love and compassion and quench their thirst to seek the truth. Just as a river does not discriminate between deserving and the undeserving, it shares its water with everybody without asking anything in return. A river simply flows and so does the enlightened Master, who has become one with the infinite source of life. By sharing his light, the Master does not lose anything; rather he becomes manifold. And when his disciples also become illumined, it proves the true enlightenment of the Master.

The Bauls of Bengal go on singing, "*Come beloved, come.*"

Osho says that they go on extending their invitations.

Love is nothing but an opening, a receptivity, a welcome, an invitation, to say, "*I am ready; come, please.*"

The Master is a host; he refuses nobody. True masters never refuse anybody. They cannot. If they start refusing people, then there is no hope. If you go under a tree, a shady tree — tired of your journey and the burning sun on your head — and the tree refuses you; it does not give you refuge, it does not shelter you. This never happens. The tree is always ready to give you shelter, its shadow, its fruits, its flowers and its fragrance.

Love Thy Neighbour and Thy Enemy

We in India, celebrate Diwali, the festival of lights, with all the pomp and show. We witness the multi-coloured light coming out of the lamps and dazzling our eyes. One can hear sounds of all kinds of firecrackers at every step. Children enjoy these loud reverberations and derive joy in shocking the elders by bursting their fire-crackers, specially by catching them unawares.

To the mature and intelligent, this whole scene of fireworks and sounds is simply a nuisance, a noise and pollution. It is something very unhealthy and also risky, as we know that these fire-crackers do hurt and kill people. But these events continue next week and again next year for many more years to come, but for just one day in a year. But for those big, rich kids, this kind of dangerous Diwali has been going on for the last few weeks.

These kids have been throwing bombs on the people of small nations thinking that by bringing darkness and death to the people of the poor countries they could celebrate light in their life. Little do they realise that at times even the worm can turn and revolt. Then much greater harm will be caused to those who incite trouble.

There's a strange rule and mysterious wisdom in life: Your enemy changes you more than your friend. By fighting with your enemy, you become like your enemy. So you can choose anybody as your friend, but you have to be very careful about choosing your enemy, because in your fight with your enemy you are bound to become like him.

Osho reminds of the very significant insightful message of Jesus.

Jesus says: "Love thy neighbour as thyself" — again and again. And he also says: "Love thy enemy as thyself." And if you analyse both the sentences together, you will find that the neighbour and the enemy are almost always the same person. "Love thy neighbour as thyself" and "Love thy enemy as thyself" — what does he mean?

He simply means that don't have any barriers for your compassion, for your love. As you love yourself, love the entire existence, because in the ultimate analysis, the whole existence is yourself. It is you who gets reflected in many mirrors. It is you who is not separate from you. Your neighbour is just a form of you; your enemy is also a form of you. Whatsoever and whosoever you come across, you come across yourself. You may not recognise this phenomenon because you are not very alert; you may not be able to see yourself in the other, but then something is wrong with your vision, something is wrong with your eyes.

Compassion is therapeutic, according to Osho. Meditation leads to compassion and one rises above hate and enmity. "Compassion is an inner air-conditioning. Suddenly everything is cool and beautiful, and nothing can disturb you, and the whole existence is transformed into a friend. Now there are no more enemies... because when you look through the eyes of anger, somebody becomes an enemy; when you look through the eyes of compassion, everybody is a friend, a neighbour. When you love, everywhere is God; when you hate, everywhere is the devil. It is your standpoint that is projected onto reality."

Only Love

Once a disciple asked Osho: "In the East, it has been stressed one should stay with a person, one person, in a love relationship. In the West, now people float from one relationship to another. Which do you favour?"

Osho replied: "Love."

Let me explain: Be true to love, and don't bother about the number of partners. The question is if you are true to love, if you live with a woman or man and don't love him, you live in sin. If you are married to somebody and don't love that person but make love to him or her, you are committing sin against love... and love is God. You are deciding against love for social convenience. It is as wrong as raping a woman you don't love. It is a crime because you don't love the woman and she does not love you. The same thing happens if you live with a woman and don't love her. Then it is rape — socially accepted, but rape nevertheless.

If you remain true to love, it is one of the most beautiful things to remain with one person, because intimacy grows. But there are 99 per cent possibilities that there is no love. You only live together.

But it is possible that if you love someone and live your life with him or her, intimacy will grow and love will have deeper revelations. This is not possible if you change partners. It is as if you keep changing a tree from one place to another. It never grows roots. Intimacy is good, and to remain in one commitment is beautiful, but love is necessary. In the West, people are changing — too many relationships. Love is killed both ways. In the East it is killed because people are afraid to change; in the West it is killed because people are afraid of commitment. So before it becomes this, change.

I am in favour of love. Always remember: If it is a love relationship, good. While love lasts, remain as deeply committed as possible. Be absorbed by the relationship. Love will transform you. If there is no love, change.

But don't become an addict of change like buying a new car. Suddenly, you come across a new woman, it is not very different. A woman is a woman, the way a man is a man. In each woman all women are represented, and in each man all men are represented. The differences are superficial: The nose is a little longer or shorter; hair is blond or brunette. The question is of female and male energy. So if love is there, stick to it. Give it a chance to grow. Or else, change.

A young wife in the confessional asked the priest about contraceptives. "You must not use them," said the priest. "They are against God's law. Take a glass of water."

"Before, or after?" asked the wife.

"Instead!" replied the priest. You ask whether to follow the Eastern way or the Western way. Neither; you follow the divine way. Remain true to love.

Stay Tuned

Human beings and their minds are complex phenomena. Psychologists have been trying to understand them but it needs an enlightened mind to penetrate humanity's collective consciousness. In the *Path of the Mystic*, Osho reveals fascinating secrets. He says: "We are living in a network of invisible forces that connect us to each other. So, whenever something happens to one, it vibrates the others. They may be far away but if it happens to many, vibrations are very strong. It can travel from one island to another, one continent to another, without visible means of communication."

Albert Einstein was once asked that if he had not discovered the theory of relativity, did he think it would have ever been discovered? He said, "If I hadn't discovered it, someone else would have. I was just quick enough." Later, it was found that a German physicist had already reached the conclusion on the theory in his notebooks; he was just late in publishing it. Another Japanese scientist was nearing end of his research on the same topic but was completely unaware of what was happening in the other part of the world. Moreover, it was difficult for him as he didn't understand English or German. But he also had reached the same conclusion. All it needed was the final touch.

It seems whenever something is happening, it doesn't happen to one. There is a wave. Whoever catches it, whoever is capable and intelligent will get the same idea. No discovery depends on an individual. It becomes attached to the individual's name because he is the first one to achieve it. Because it is a specialised subject, not everyone will be able to discover it, but there are many in the same field, with similar specialisations. And if a certain wave surrounds the earth, it is likely to be caught by many minds.

Osho talks about a practical experiment we could do. He said: "You can sit in another room separate from someone with whom you have a loving relationship, a trust, something of the heart. Both should sit for 10 minutes in silence. Then decide that a person takes a card from a pack and makes a signal — may be a knock on the door — that 'the first card has been taken; now you take a card.' It's the other person's turn next. He has to be silent and in tune, open to what is happening next door. This way, take 10 one by one. If both are intelligent, seven cards will be the same.

"This is the minimum; all the 10 cards can be same. Even if three are same, all that's needed are more experiments for it to grow. And you can do it with other things. Draw a picture, and the other will sketch the same, minus visible communication as something invisible reaches them. Change partners and you'll see with whom it functions better. It means your minds operates on the same wavelength.

In my opinion, before two persons decide to live together they should check if their minds are in tune. They should be at least 70 per cent in tune, only then is it worth living together; otherwise, don't create hell for each other. You love each other — forgive each other."

STAY TUNED

But you can try to improve attunement before living together. No need to move the court because what can a magistrate do?

This is something that should be a part of a university — there should be a department helping people find how attuned to each other they are, and helping to increase attunement. If they are so far apart it seems impossible, suggest, "You'll get in trouble. If you love each other... don't. It is better to say goodbye now than after messing up." This can be extended around the earth.

First try it in one house with 10 people and if you find a common wavelength, spread it around. They should start an experiment at the same time, and the results will be the same. Percentage will also be the same because distance makes no difference.

Buddha

Meditation is a flower. It has roots. It exists in you. Once compassion happens, it is not rooted; it simply moves and goes on moving. Buddha has disappeared but not his compassion. The flower will die sooner or later -- it is part of earth and the dust will return unto dust -- but the fragrance that has been released will remain forever and forever. Buddha has gone, Jesus has gone, but not their fragrance. Their compassion still continues and whoever is open to their compassion will immediately feel its impact, will be moved by it, will be taken on a new journey, on a new pilgrimage.

—Osho

Buddha: Full Moon of Enlightenment

The world celebrates Gautam Buddha's birthday on the full moon day in summer. It is said that he was born, attained enlightenment and left his body in the final *nirvana* on the night of the full moon. Buddha is the full moon of enlightenment. In fact, 25 centuries after the birth of the Buddha, his enlightenment and the Buddha himself have really become synonymous.

Our world has known so many sages and mystics before Gautam Buddha as the enlightened one, but it was only Gautam Buddha who has become identified with this title. There's something special about Gautam Buddha. Not only did he attain enlightenment under a Bodhi tree; he himself became a huge tree of enlightenment, with thousands of branches, inviting the seekers of truth to seek enlightenment.

Buddha became such an ocean of enlightenment, such an infinite source that hundreds of streams started flowing from this source. Since then thousands of illumined Buddhist and Zen masters who appeared on the scene, have their roots in the Buddha.

Buddha never preached about God; actually he avoided this much worn out word as himself being called Bhagwan, the Blessed

One. Oscar Wilde described him the most godless yet the most godly.

Buddha warned us against idol-worship, yet his statues and idols are seen everywhere in the world. A single temple in Japan has got ten thousand idols. All these idols manifest nothing but various expressions and manifestations of enlightenment. These artistic expressions are not meant for worship but meditation. The world had not seen such an enlightened face of meditation before. Buddha became meditation personified.

And the Buddha's luminous face reminds us of our hidden original face, the Buddhahood within. It reminds us to forget God outside and remember the Buddha within ourselves if we wish to realise godliness.

What the Buddha preached was something totally paradoxical and unique. Osho calls it a "religionless religion, which is not religion but religiousness."

Says Osho about the Buddha: "I love Gautam Buddha because he represents to me the essential core of religion. He is a beginner of a totally different kind of religion in the world. He is founder of a religionless religion. He has propounded not religion but religiousness; and this is a great radical change in the history of human consciousness."

Buddha is the ultimate liberator, who liberated religion from the rotten ancient labels and gave it a fresh beginning and a new life. His religiousness is throbbing with all the life force and youthfulness today, even after 25 centuries.

Buddha was not our contemporary, and the world has not evolved so much as to become contemporary of the Buddha. He still remains ahead of our time. We have to evolve our consciousness to become his contemporary. We have to become enlightened ones ourselves, and only then we can think of ourselves as his contemporary. We will have to meditate and raise the level of our consciousness to his level. He functions as a radiant reminder for all of us who are on the path.

Osho says in a discourse on Bodhidharma, the greatest Zen Master: "Remember, by 'Buddha' is not meant any personal name. 'Buddha' simply means the awakened one. Anyone who becomes awakened, enlightened, is the Buddha. You are also the Buddha; the only difference is that you are not aware of it. You have never looked inside yourself and found the Buddha there. Your very life source is nothing but enlightenment."

194

Buddha's Message

Scientific knowledge in the world has its own tradition. Osho tells us about this tradition: "...scientific truths, once discovered, become the property of everybody else. Albert Einstein worked hard for 13 years to discover the theory of relativity; now you can read all about it within hours — you need not discover it again. Edison worked for years, at least for three years, to discover the first electric light bulb; now you can go on producing electric light bulbs — you don't need an Edison to produce them. Ordinary labourers know nothing of electricity but can do the job — they are doing it."

Those earlier scientists did not make billions. Because all their inventions and discoveries have been a gift to the whole world; the science of the total health of the *yoga sutras* has been available to the whole world without any restrictions. Shiva gave 112 techniques of Tantra and the world has been benefiting from this inner science without ever feeling a need of any trademark or patent.

In the East it is believed that whatever comes in the realm of science and knowledge should remain an open source and everybody should be welcome to drink from the fountain of knowledge. Knowledge is a liberating phenomenon. *Upanishads* declare: "*Sa vidya ya vimuktaye* — knowledge liberates." The true knowledge is of universal nature and is meant for the liberation of whole mankind.

Osho once said, "I would like you to be enriched by Newton, Edison, Eddington, Rutherford, Einstein and I would also like you to be enriched by the Buddha, Krishna, Christ, Mohammed, so that you can become rich in both the dimensions — the outer and the inner. Science is good as far as it goes, but it does not go far enough — and it cannot go. I am not saying that it can go and it does not go. No, it CANNOT go into the interiority of your being. The very methodology of science prevents it from going in. It can go only outwards; it can study only objectively; it cannot go into the subjectivity itself. That is the function of religion.

"The society needs science; the society needs religion. And if you ask me what should be the first priority — science should be the first priority. First the outer — the circumference, then the inner, because the inner is more subtle, more delicate. Science can create the real space for religion to exist on earth."

About knowledge he quotes, " '*Sa vidya vimuktaye* — knowledge is that which liberates.' This is the most original definition of knowledge. This is the definition of knowledge as well as its criterion."

Osho advocates against copyrighting of knowledge and said, "Things can be copyrighted, thoughts cannot be copyrighted, and certainly meditation cannot be copyrighted. They are not things of the marketplace. For ten thousand years the East has been meditating and nobody has put trademarks upon meditation."

Gautam Buddha's birthday is celebrated in India as Buddha Purnima day. He was the benevolent friend of humanity, who gifted the world with *Vipassana* among other things. Let us celebrate his birthday as also all the other days with his meditation and remind the whole world that there should be total freedom in the knowledge of inner and outer science.

The Real *Jihad*

Their job is to kill. They kill others. They kill themselves. According to them they do it for their religion and they call it *jihad*!

Their *jihad* never ends. It has been going on since man started thinking and believing — that what is right for him is right for others too. This belief created a self-righteous attitude and superiority complex of holier-than-thou feeling. Those who do not share this belief become sinners or *kafirs* who have no right to live and must be eliminated. This *jihad* has not been prevalent only in one particular religion — it has been flourishing in all the religions that teach belief but not reason.

So there's a jihad of belief and *jihad* of reasoning. I would choose a better word for second type of *jihad* — the *jihad* of consciousness, which sees consciousness in all the beings and has compassion for all. It is a *jihad* of reverence for all life — in all the forms. This *jihad* has nothing to do with killing — this *jihad* saves life and has reverence. This *jihad* of self-transformation begins at the individual level of self-purification; getting rid of all evil thoughts and ill will towards others. This *jihad* is very different and remarkable for the fact that it happens in the realm of soul. Sufis call this *jihad*, the *jihadun-Nafs*. It is the intimate struggle to purify the soul of evil influence. It is the struggle to cleanse one's spirit of sin. This in fact is the real *jihad* of self-transformation — all other *jihads* are childish.

Osho would narrate a story of a killer bandit, Angulimal, who was also on some kind of *jihad*. This ferocious killer used to kill people and wear a garland of their fingers and thus came to be notoriously known as Angulimal. Nobody knew his real name. Gautam Buddha was passing through the deserted jungle where this man used to rob and kill people. His disciples warned him not to go that way, because he had taken a vow to kill one hundred people. He had already killed 99 persons. He needed to kill only one person more. Now even if he saw his mother, he would kill her.

Buddha said, "If you had not told me, then I may have gone by the other road. But now that I know that he is waiting for one person only and nobody is willing to go, not even his mother, then if I don't go, what is going to happen to his vow? And I am going to die anyway sooner or later, so let him fulfil his vow. And who knows whether he will be able to kill me or I will be able to kill him?"

Angulimal saw Gautam Buddha coming. He was not aware of who this man was, but something was beautiful about this man; the way he was coming, the joy, the peace, the silence. And when the Buddha came in front of him he said to the Buddha, "Please, you go. I am a dangerous man. It seems you don't know about me. You look so innocent. I am Angulimal! I can see that you are a *sannyasin* — your yellow robe, your shaved head. I feel a strange compassion for you I have never felt, so I will give you one chance. You can go back and I will wait for somebody else, but if you insist, if you even take a single step ahead, I am going to kill you."

Buddha asked, "Do you know me? If that is your vow, then this is my vow: I never go back. You kill me!"

The man drew out his sword, but his hand trembled. Buddha said, "What is the matter? Is this the way? Are you a swordsman? Your hand is trembling! Stop your hand from trembling! This is not right — this shows weakness. One should be strong enough. And I am surprised and I am wondering how you could kill so many people."

Angulimal said, "This is for the first time. My heart is beating faster, my breathing is no more rhythmic, and my hand is trembling. You must be doing something! You seem to be a magician!"

Buddha replied, "That is true — I am also trying my way, I am trying to kill you! But I don't kill physically; I kill psychologically! But you finish your job; don't bother about my work. I will go on doing my work and you carry on your own. But before you hit my body, one thing you have to do for me — this is my last wish of a dying man. Can you cut a few leaves from the tree?"

Those leaves were just hanging on top of them. Angulimal cut a small branch and gave it to the Buddha. Buddha said, "Good, half is done. Now do the other half — join this branch back again and then kill me."

Angulimal said, "You must be mad! How can I join it back?"

Buddha replied, "But cutting a branch even a child can do. The real thing is joining it. Destruction is very easy; creation is the real thing. Are you a man or a child?"

Angulimal bowed down his head, ashamed. Buddha said, "If

you can understand that much, then there is no problem, I would love to be murdered by you — you kill me."

Angulimal threw down his sword, fell at Buddha's feet and said, "You have killed me before I could kill you. You are right — destruction can be done by anybody. Now teach me how to be creative."

The real *jihad* is purity, creativity and compassion.

Make Work Your Worship

Once Bodhidharma, an outrageous and outspoken Buddhist monk from India, went to China, where he was greeted by the emperor with fanfare. His name and fame had reached China and people were awaiting the arrival of the disciple of the Buddha. The emperor made a big show of welcoming Bodhidharma to make an impression on his people that he was also a very religious person. After welcoming him, the emperor asked the monk: "Bhante, please answer some of my questions. I have got hundreds of dharamshalas and temples built for the Buddhist monks so that they can relax and meditate comfortably. What shall be my reward in heaven?"

Bodhidharma said, "You will go to hell directly. This will be the reward of all that you have done."

The emperor was disturbed. But he had no idea how the real sages behaved. He had seen only those monks who ran after the rich and powerful. This is mutual exploitation. The ordinary monks and sadhus also want recognition from the rich and powerful to show to their followers how great they are and the rich people want to maintain their social status and keep such monks happy.

Bodhidharma shocked the emperor but it was the most enlightening statement that showed the emperor the true path of meditation.

Most of the creative people are always seeking all kinds of national and international awards and only a few of them get such awards. The others feel frustrated. But what the people don't realise is that to be creative is a reward unto itself.

Osho says: "There is no God for me except this existence, which is so utterly beautiful that work with love is bound to become your worship. In worship the worker is lost completely, only the worship remains. Digging a ditch in your garden, making food for those you love, or anything else, if you are lost in it so utterly that there is no ego or even its shadow left — you have become your work. I want worship to become your 24 hour-a-day thing. It has to become existential. Then you don't need to go to any church, to any synagogue."

203

True Spirit of Hedonism

Osho shares his vision of the 'new man' for the current millennium before leaving the earth. One expression he used frequently was 'Zorba the Buddha'. Zorba is a character from the novel, *Zorba the Greek*, written by Nikos Kazantzakis.

In the novel, Zorba's whole life is a life of simple, physical enjoyment without any anxiety, guilt or preoccupation about sin and virtue. He represents a life of worldly joys. Buddha represents the life of inner joys.

Osho brings the two together in his vision of the 'new man'. For him, the inner and the outer are not two. The inner is the inner of the outer, and the outer is the outer of the inner. He said: "The body has to be enjoyed as much as your soul. Matter has its own beauty, its own power, just as consciousness has its own world, its own silence, its own peace, its own ecstasy. And between the two is the area of the mind — something of matter and something of the spirit. The poet is just in the middle, between the materialist and the spiritualist; his poetry touches both extremes. I would like all the three points — the two extremes and the middle — to become one unity."

Osho defines the 'new man' as the holy man: One who is whole and not divided or schizophrenic. He exhorted his followers to spread this new vision of a 'new man': "We have to propagate the idea to everyone who have ears to hear and eyes to see, and any intelligence to understand the clear-cut alternative. You create a new kind of religiousness that has never existed before — earthly, physical; not against the spirit but in tune with the spiritual. That's what I mean by Zorba the Buddha."

A man who rejoices in his body and the wisdom of the body, a man who uses his mind as a tremendously significant mechanism that evolution has brought, and a man who does not stop at mind but goes on searching beyond, into the realms of divineness, into the realms of godliness — to produce this man should be the effort of all those who are in some way concerned with educating the new generation. "The educationists, the journalists, the spiritual teachers — all people who are involved in some way in creating a better human being than has been possible in the past — have to accept the totality of man without rejecting anything," says Osho.

Zorba the Buddha heralds a new consciousness for a brave new world and seeks an end to all the conflicts that have been dividing the humanity. Osho's Zorba the Buddha on the one hand, is the end of the old man — his religions, his politics, his nations, his racial discriminations, and all kinds of stupidities. On the other hand, Zorba the Buddha is the beginning of a new man — a man totally free to be himself, allowing his nature to blossom.

There is no conflict between Zorba and the Buddha. The conflict has been created by the so-called religions. Is there any conflict between your body and your soul? Is there any conflict between your life and your consciousness? Is there any conflict between your right hand and your left hand? They are all one in an organic unity.

TRUE SPIRIT OF HEDONISM

Your body is not something to be condemned but something to be grateful for, because it is the greatest thing in existence, the most miraculous; its workings are just unbelievable. It has no conflict and moves in some inner synchronicity, always together. And your soul is not something opposed to your body. If your body is the house, the soul is your guest. And there is no need for the guest and the host to continuously fight. But religions could not exist without you fighting with yourself.

"My insistence on your organic unity, so that your materialism is no longer opposed to spiritualism, is basically to demolish all religions from the earth. Once your body and soul start moving hand in hand, dancing together, you have become Zorba the Buddha. Then you can enjoy everything of this life, everything that is outside you, and you can also enjoy everything that is within you," says Osho.

Osho's 'new man' has a totally new approach towards life. He lives an undivided life of love and laughter, meditation and transformation, creativity and compassion. He lives moment to moment with awareness and bliss. He squeezes the juice from each moment in life.

Osho has added a new dimension to spirituality. "Allow me to coin the term 'spiritual hedonism', because ordinarily you think of hedonism as very earthy. 'Eat, drink, be merry' — that is earthy hedonism. In spiritual hedonism that is there, and more also. 'Eat, drink, be merry' is there, plus God. A spiritual hedonism is always there when religion is alive. When the religion becomes dead, hedonism disappears completely and the religion becomes antagonistic to everything that man can enjoy. Only a new religion — just born, fresh, original — can celebrate. Then celebration fits with it. It can love, can trust, can enjoy."

The Masters and the Mystics

Life needs a balance between the depth and the height. I teach you both simultaneously. In your entering to the center in meditation, you are growing your roots deeper into the cosmos. And bringing the buddha out from the hidden center is bringing your fragrance, bringing your grace, bringing your ecstasy higher, where it can blossom into the sky.

Your ecstasy is a movement towards the height and your meditation is a movement towards the depth. And once you have both, your life becomes a celebration.

That is my work, to transform your life from a sad affair into a celebration.

—Osho

Guru: God-man and Man-God

India celebrates Ashadh Purnima, the full moon of July as Guru Purnima, the day when all disciples come together to express their gratitude towards their guru. This is something uniquely Indian. It is unlike a student-teacher relationship, which is very formal. A teacher imparts knowledge to students and gets paid for it. A guru does not merely impart knowledge to his disciples; he shares his being and illumination with them. Disciples learn the deeper meaning of life by living in guru's presence. The guru does not have to teach with his words; he guides with his own life. Hence a teacher does not command the same love and respect that a guru does; the teacher does not deserve it. Teachers often complain that their students are not as respectful to them as they should be. Respect cannot be forcibly demanded; it has to come naturally. When a teacher evolves into a guru, he commands natural respect — not just respect, but love and devotion too. The disciple becomes so devoted to the guru that he can sacrifice his life for him, though a true guru never expects any sacrifice. The guru shares his being, his love and light with his disciples unconditionally.

Something about the meaning of the word 'guru'. 'Gu' means darkness and 'ru' means dispeller. One who dispels darkness is your guru. The first basic requirement of living with guru is meditation. Meditation is not a few deep breathing exercises; it is a way of life. Meditation is the medicine for all the social sicknesses that people suffer from. That's why these two words — meditation and medicine — have the same root: *medi*. The guru gives this medicine of meditation to his disciples and makes them healthy. Talking about this health, Osho explains that Sanskrit word for healthy is *'swastha'*. *'Swa'* means self and *'stha'* means rooted. You become healthy when you become rooted in your self. You are sick when you lose connection with your self, your own being. Meditation reconnects you with your self and makes you healthy. That's why it can be called a medicine. And the man who gives you this medicine is the real guru, a *sadguru*. The mystic saint Kabir gives more respect to the *sadguru* than to God himself.

Osho says: "There is a story about Kabir that when he arrived home and faced God, he was very much puzzled because the guru was standing there with God. He was puzzled about whom he should bow down to first, the priority — to God, or to the guru? And then he touched the feet of the guru and said, 'Because without you, I would have never known God. So you come first. Through you I have known God; so you come first. God can wait, because without you there was no God for me. It is only through you he has become a reality. I bow down to you'."

Kabir says, "The guru is great beyond words, and great is the good fortune of the disciple." There are millions of people; very few become seekers. There are thousands of seekers; very few become disciples. To become a disciple is a rare privilege because only by becoming a disciple does one become connected, linked, with a Master. Then your destiny is not alone; then your destiny is linked with a Master.

GURU: GOD-MAN AND MAN-GOD

The inner journey of truth begins with the help of a Master who has already attained to the truth.

The illumination of the Master becomes an invitation to the unlit lamp of the disciple who gropes in the dark, looking for somebody who can show him the way. To find such a Master is really a blessing, a benediction. Half of the inner journey is over by meeting such a Master and the other half is over when the disciple comes to fruition and becomes a Master himself.

Somebody asks Osho: "Who are you?"

Osho replies: "I am an invitation. I am an invitation for all those who are seeking, searching, and have a deep longing in their hearts to find their home."

A true enlightened Master is an open invitation to one and all, without any discrimination of caste, colour or creed. He invites everybody to come and drink from the river of his wisdom, love and compassion and quench their thirst to seek the truth. Just as a river does not discriminate between deserving and the undeserving, it shares its water with everybody without asking anything in return. A river simply flows and so does the enlightened Master, who has become one with the infinite source of life. By sharing his light, the Master does not lose anything; rather it becomes manifold. And when his disciples also become illumined, it proves the true enlightenment of the Master.

The Bauls of Bengal go on singing, "*Come beloved, come.*"

Osho says that they go on extending their invitation.

Love is nothing but an opening, a receptivity, a welcome, an invitation, to say, "I am ready; come, please."

The Master is a host; he refuses nobody. True masters never

refuse anybody. They cannot. If they start refusing people, then there is no hope. If you go under a tree, a shady tree, tired of your journey and the burning sun on your head, and the tree refuses you, it does not give you refuge, it does not shelter you? This never happens. The tree is always ready to give you shelter, its shadow, its fruits, its flowers and its fragrance.

Mystic Ways of Transformation

Religion and morality are generally understood to be the same. But, in reality they are a world apart. A religious person may be a moral person, but a moral person may not necessarily be a religious person. Religiousness is above morality.

Osho says: "A really religious person has no morality imposed upon him. His morality arises out of his consciousness. He is not trying to do the right, he is not trying to avoid the wrong — he simply acts out of his consciousness, and whatever he does is right."

Osho talks about a great mystic, Nagarjuna, who was a naked *fakir*. A queen was deeply in love with Nagarjuna. One day she invited him as a guest in her palace. Nagarjuna went. The queen asked him a favour: "I want your begging bowl." Nagarjuna gave it. The queen brought a golden begging bowl, studded with diamonds and gave it to Nagarjuna. She said, "Now you keep this. I will worship your begging bowl."

Had Nagarjuna been an ordinary mystic, he would have said: "I cannot touch it. I have renounced the world." But for him it was all the same, so he took the bowl.

When he left the palace, a thief saw him and followed.

The thief was very happy: 'Soon Nagarjuna will sleep and I will get the bowl.' Nagarjuna threw the bowl outside the door, thinking: Why make him wait?

'Such a precious thing! And Nagarjuna has thrown it so easily.' The thief could not go without thanking him. He peeked in and he said, "Sir, accept my thanks. I cannot believe that there are people like you too? Can I come in and touch your feet?"

Nagarjuna laughed and said: "Yes, that's why I threw the bowl outside."

When he touched Nagarjuna's feet, he felt the presence of the divine. He asked Nagarjuna, "How many lives will it take for me to become like you?"

Nagarjuna said, "How many lives? It can happen today, it can happen now!" The thief became his disciple.

These are the mysterious ways by which real mystics can transform even the hardened of criminals.

The Alchemy of Transformation

Anger without consciousness is, a destructive force, a suicidal force; it hurts you, it kills you by and by, it is a poison. With awareness the same energy is transformed to become compassion. The same radiance comes to your face, but not in anger — in compassion.

"The same blood flows, the same chemistry of the body, but a new foreign element has entered into it, and the whole chemistry changes," says Osho and offers a panacea for all our inner illnesses. What is that medicine? The answer is meditation.

The person who gives us this medicine of meditation is a sage, a seer, a mystic, an enlightened one or a *sadguru*. That's why the Buddha and Nanak have also described guru as *vaidya*. A guru is a *vaidya* of the inner world. He is an alchemist who knows the science of inner transformation. He gives devices to transform the baser metals into gold — the raw energy of anger and lust into finer energies of love and compassion. And in this process, you get rid of what is foreign within our system. Our consciousness, *chaitanya*, *atman*, is the real self, and all else is foreign, and to realise our real self, we have to go beyond this crude cover of baser elements of anger, jealousy, hatred, lust and violence. We have to get rid of all the foreigners dominating and ruling the inner country of our consciousness, which is in the state of deep sleep.

Osho explains: "With unconsciousness you are a base metal, with consciousness you will become gold, you are transformed. Just the fire of awareness is needed. You lack nothing else; everything is there. With the fire of awareness a new arrangement happens. You lack nothing, remember; you have everything that a Buddha needs. Just one thing is missing — and that, too, is fast asleep within you. You just have to awaken it; just a few efforts to awaken, a few efforts to become more alert."

215

The Secret of a Religious Man

J. Krishnamurti, the enlightened mystic of last century made a significant statement: "You are the world." This is one of the most powerful insights given to us by all the sages. This can transform us and bring total revolution in our life. This gives us dignity and individuality and makes us responsible human beings.

We can call ourselves individuals only when we are mature enough to accept our responsibility towards all that happens around ourselves. This is a basic spiritual approach.

The world that we are living in is in some way our own creation. If it is ugly, violent or beautiful; it is all our creation.

Osho says in the *Sermons in Stones*: "Because millions of individuals have contributed the same anger, the same hatred, the same competitiveness, the same violence, it has become mountainous. You cannot imagine that you can be responsible for it: 'I may have contributed just a small piece...' But an ocean is nothing except millions and millions of dew drops. A dew drop cannot think that it is responsible for the ocean — but the dew drop is responsible. The ocean is only a name; the reality is in the dew drop."

A Sufi poet once said: *"Main katra hi sahi, mera vajood to hai!* (So what if I am merely a drop, I do exist). The drop carries all the mysteries that an ocean has. In another context, mystic poet Kabir also said: *Bund samana samaund mein!* (Context may be different but in reality, the dew drop does represent the whole ocean).

"However small, a miniature world, but you carry all the seeds. If revolution comes to you, it heralds the revolution for the whole world. If you want to change the world, don't start by changing the world — that is the wrong way humanity has followed up to now: Change the society, change the economic structure. Change this, change that. But don't change the individual.

"That's why all revolutions have failed. Only one revolution can succeed, which has not been tried till now — and that is the revolution of the individual. You change yourself. Be alert not to contribute anything that makes the world a hell. And remember to contribute to the world something that makes it a paradise. This is the secret of a religious man. And if every individual starts following it, there will be a revolution without any bloodshed."

Kabir's Poetic Call to Celebrate Life

Not all poets are enlightened. Most of them have their poetic flights only when they are fully drunk. It is rare to find the combination of enlightenment and poetry in a person. If it is present in a person, he will be called a sage. Such a person is also drunk but drunk on the divine. Mystic Kabir was one such poet. His poems are not ordinary poems; they are simple on the surface but deeply profound. They have an element of ecstasy and madness in them. Kabir's poetry contains all contradictions, what we call *ulatbaansiyan* in Hindi language. In one of the famous *ulatbaansi*, Kabir says: *Ek achambha hamne dekha, nadiya laagi aag.* (Kabir is wonderstuck to see the miracle of a river catching fire!).

In *Ecstasy the Forgotten Language*, Osho takes us into such a wonderful world of Kabir: "I invite you to come with me into the innermost realm of this madman Kabir. Yes, he was a madman; all religious people are. Mad, because they don't trust reason. Mad, because they love life. Mad, because they can dance and sing. Mad, because to them life is not a question, not a problem to be solved but a mystery into which one has to dissolve oneself."

Kabir shared his ultimate experience of the divine by singing his songs and dancing in ecstasy. He did not write poetry; he became poetry and it was flowing from his being. Osho says: "This is a spontaneous outpouring of his heart.

"He was a singer, he was a poet: Somebody would ask something and he would sing a song spontaneously. And nobody has ever sung such songs. He celebrates all. What he is going to say to you is not philosophy but pure poetry. It is not religion but a hand beckoning, a door half opened, a mirror wiped clean. It is a way back home, a way back to nature."

Nature is God to Kabir. He did not believe in temples, churches and mosques; he believed in the living reality. God is there, breathing, flowering, flowing.

There has always been a conflict between man-made temples of worship. We cannot blame the temples for this conflict. It is the human mind that has been polluting these places of worship. Kabir calls you back from such temples and mosques. He calls you back to nature to celebrate life.

Mysteries of Master-Disciple Relationship

Osho talks about Sufis who have an interesting story highlighting this relationship. Sufi Master Junnaid, a seeker, used to tell his disciples, "When I met my Master, he never looked at me for three years. But I was persistent. I stayed there right in front of him."

After three years the Master looked at him for the first time. That was the recognition that he was not a student, but a disciple. A student would have got lost in three years; no student can stay that long waiting just for a look. Then another three years passed and he never looked again.

After three years the Master looked again and smiled. His smile cut through the heart of Junnaid, who wondered why he had smiled. But the Master did not give him a chance to ask. He started talking to other disciples. After another three years, he called him and kissed his forehead. "My son, now you are ready. Now you can go and spread the message."

But he hadn't been given any message. He couldn't figure out what the message could be. But if the Master was urging him to go, he would have to. So, touching his Master's feet, Junnaid left for his mission.

A Master kissing the devotee is a declaration that the merger (between the Master and disciple) has taken place. Osho explains that a spiritual seeker passes through three stages in life — student, disciple and devotee. The student is unconscious. The disciple starts becoming conscious. The devotee is so conscious that he cannot be conscious of his consciousness.

It has to be a recognition from the Master because from the devotee the distance between himself and the Master is nil. From the devotee one grows into a Master, but it is a spontaneous and natural growth.

A Spiritual Pathbreaker

Guru Gorakh Nath, though not as well-known as Guru Nanak, Sant Kabir or Meera Bai, is a rare saint that this country has produced. He can be credited with being a pathbreaker in the mysterious world of spirituality, who created several powerful devices to attain self-realisation. He was the master of various types of *siddhis*, which are essential for ultimate enlightenment. Interestingly, the word in Hindi, *gorakhdhandha* had been coined in his memory. Though sometimes it is used negatively, it was originally meant to convey the innumerable ways of attaining enlightenment. Gorakh Nath experimented with all the ways and created a sort of science of spirituality. The saints after him owe him a lot.

According to Osho: "Gorakh is the first link in a chain. Through him a new type of religion was born. Without Gorakh, there could be no Kabir, Nanak, Dadu, Vajid, Farid or Meera — without Gorakh none of them are possible. The basic root of all of them is in Gorakh. Since then the temple has been built high. On this temple many golden spires have been raised. Though the golden spires may be seen from afar, they cannot be more important than the foundation stone. The foundation is not visible to anyone, but on this very stone stands the whole structure. The peaks are worshipped. People simply forget about the foundation. Gorakh has been similarly forgotten."

Though Gorakh Nath is popularly known as a *tantrik*, in reality he was much more than that. Osho says that he made many discoveries about the inner life of man, perhaps more than anyone else. He pushed open so many doors that would lead to the inner being of a man. One can always say that he had a rare personality, something similar to Einstein. Just as the great scientist provided so many methods for investigating the truth of the universe, similarly Gorakh Nath came up with new methods to realise one's potential. Of all the methods that Gorakh Nath taught, what is most remarkable is his approach of taking meditation lightly and not so seriously. He says:

Laughing, playing, the knack of meditation,
day and night sharing divine knowledge.
He laughs, plays, keeps mind untroubled,
such unwavering one is always with God.

223

Spirit Wants to be One with Universe

There is a saying: 'Ego wants to rule the universe, spirit wants to be one with it.' Ego thinks and in thinking it deludes itself that it is so powerful that it can rule the world. It is just like a wave that thinks it can rule the whole ocean. This is unthinkable and unimaginable. But our ego does think and imagine this way and leads us to unnecessary struggle and misery. Why this happens is a puzzle. In Zen terminology we can call it a *koan*, a riddle that cannot be solved by the rational mind. 'What is the sound of one hand clapping?" a disciple is asked. He thinks, contemplates and meditates. After many attempts, he experiences the answer as a clear reflection of the truth and with it comes a realisation.

There is another *koan*: "If you meet the Buddha on the way, kill him!" No, how can a disciple kill his Master who is no longer in his body? Buddha left his body 25 centuries ago. Where will he meet the Buddha now and how will he kill him? And why should he kill him?

Osho explains this *koan* as follows: "It is a message to the disciple who loves the Buddha so much that there is a possibility that the Buddha may become his last barrier—because of his love, because he is a disciple, because he is a *sannyasin*, because he meditates, goes deeper and deeper into his being and will feel more and more grateful towards the Buddha. But, the Master has to be left behind at the last moment; you have to say goodbye to him too. Remember this is something internal. When all thoughts disappear, then only one thought remains—the thought of your Master. And it is very difficult to say goodbye. You owe so much to the Master—he has been your source, your transformation; he has been your nourishment, your life; he has brought you along the long way. And to say goodbye to the person who has been your guide, your friend? He has been a constant companion in the dark night of the soul; and now when the dawn is coming, you say goodbye to him? It seems impossible! And the disciple, at the last moment, starts clinging to the idea of the Master."

This is a mysterious phenomenon that only happens in a Master-disciple relationship. So the first thing is to become a disciple, become committed and dedicated to the Master, so that the spiritual journey begins. One starts moving inwards, reaches the ultimate point and the moment comes when one finds his Master still there within. At this point one needs to say goodbye to the Master. And then the spirit becomes one with the universe.

Guru-Disciple Relationship is Beyond Time

An oft-asked question is: "Does a guru who is no longer in his physical body help his disciples on their spiritual journey and growth in consciousness?" There is always a big debate on this subject — and the answer to this question is both 'yes' and 'no'. Even after his departure from this world, a guru is always available to his disciple, provided he is a real disciple and the guru is a genuine guru.

Primarily, it all depends on the receptivity and the understanding of the disciple and his love and devotion to the guru. If the disciple is just a student merely interested in collecting informative knowledge and enhancing his ego, he will not be able to receive any help from the guru. His ego will function as a barrier between him and his guru. It is only when the disciple is able to surrender his ego, he becomes receptive to the inner treasures of enlightenment a guru has to offer.

The guru is originally an eastern phenomenon. Osho explains: "There is no word in English to translate the word guru because the relationship between guru and disciple is basically eastern. No such relationship has ever existed in western culture and tradition, so no one in the West can understand what a guru is. At the most they can understand what a teacher is."

A guru becomes a guru only after he has attained self-realisation and enlightenment. Before that he may just be a teacher but not a guru.

A guru transforms his disciples with his presence. And when the guru disappears physically, he becomes even more available because then there is no physical barrier — his 'unembodied' consciousness becomes available to the disciple in his meditation.

In one of his discourses, Osho assures his disciples: "So remember, when I am gone, you are not going to lose anything. Perhaps you may gain something of which you are absolutely unaware. Right now I am available to you only embodied, imprisoned in a certain shape and form. When I am gone, where can I go? I will be here in the winds, in the ocean; and if you have loved me, if you have trusted me, you will feel me in a thousand and one ways. In your silent moments, you will suddenly feel my presence. One I am unembodied, my consciousness is universal. Right now, you have to come to me."

In Search of an Eternal India

Come, let us meditate on India. India seems to have forgotten what India really is. The country that gave birth to the enlightened mystics is today among the top contenders for being the most corrupt nation of the world.

Sages, saints and mystics born in this part of the world had collectively envisaged an India very different from what it is today. They envisioned India and its people as the meditators and the seekers of truth.

The *Upanishads* declared: "*Amritasya putrah!* Oh sons of the eternal and immortal! Wake up!" Osho says that only those who have heard this clarion call and are on this *amrit path*— the eternal path, are the real citizens of India. People accidentally born here are not the real citizens.

Osho assays that the person who was involved in the search of self-realisation and truth, irrespective of the place he was born in, was the real resident of India. For Osho, India and spirituality were synonymous: India and *sanatan dharma*, the eternal stream of religiousness are synonymous. Hence, the sons of India are actually everywhere on the earth. And those who happen to be living here but are not madly in search of the immortal have no right to be called Indians.

Osho declares that India is an eternal pilgrimage — a *sanatan yatra* — an immortal path spreading from eternity to eternity. The India of this spirit needs to be awakened again for herself and the world. It should play a pivotal role in this resurgence. Humanity has no future if India disappears in the darkness.

India's destiny is the destiny of the whole humanity. The rise of consciousness, the light of enlightenment, the blossoming of flowers of meditation and their fragrances in the form of love and compassion that has blessed this part of the earth has never been experienced so much anywhere else.

This is because of the non-stop search for truth, yoga and meditation which has kept the flame burning. A powerful reminder is needed urgently!

"India is not just geography or history. It is not only a nation, a country, a mere piece of land. It is something more: It is a metaphor, poetry, something invisible but very tangible. It is vibrating with certain energy fields which no other country can claim. For almost ten thousand years, thousands of people have reached to the ultimate explosion of consciousness. Their vibration is still alive, their impact is in the very air; you just need a certain perceptivity, a certain capacity to receive the invisible that surrounds this strange land," says the Master in *Osho Upanishad*.

To be Ordinary is Very Extraordinary

It is said that Sant Dadu Dayal used to pray and sing devotional songs sitting alone in his hut. Once a policeman visited him and inquired about him from a man clearing thorns outside the hut. But his tone was arrogant. The man, who was asked the question, continued with his cleaning and singing without replying. The policeman was infuriated and asked another person, even more arrogantly: "Where does Dadu Dayal live?"

The man responded with a smile, "The person who is clearing the thorns outside the hut is Daduji."

On hearing this the policeman was left embarrassed. He took an oath that he would never speak arrogantly.

The real saints are simple and unpretentious people. Often it is difficult to recognise them and for people who are arrogant, it is impossible to recognise these saints. Kabir and Dadu belong to this category of saints, who were instrumental in bringing a spiritual revolution in the lives of their disciples.

In his book, *The Books I have Loved*, Osho paid tribute to Dadu: "Another Indian mystic, you may not have heard about him. He was called Dadu, which means the brother. There are thousands of songs that Dadu sang, but they were not written down by him; they were collected by others, just like a gardener collects flowers long fallen. I have spoken on him. He reaches to the very heights one can aspire to."

Dadu is just like Zen masters in Japan, who also lives ordinary lives. They don't live any sort of extraordinary life, because they say, "The search to be extraordinary is egoistic."

Osho says: "Just to be ordinary is the real attitude of a religious man. And remember the urge to be extraordinary is very ordinary. There is nothing extraordinary about it because everybody wants to be extraordinary. To be ordinary is very extraordinary — because who wants to be ordinary?"

Zen

A real prayer is simply prayer. It has no words; it is pure silence. It is a surrender in deep silence. In fact, it is not addressed to any God; it is bowing down to the whole existence. It is not an address. God is everywhere, all is God, so you simply bow down in tremendous gratitude, in ecstasy, in joy, in love.

—Osho

The Way of Zen: Just Being

Marjorie Hansen, the author of *The Confident Woman* used a very interesting phrase for people in her book. She calls them 'human doings' rather than 'human beings'.

The enlightened mystics of the East have also talked about these two categories. Doing is our *karma*, and being is our consciousness. From the moment we get up in the morning to the moment we hit the bed at night, we remain engaged in all kinds of doings. And when we sleep, our minds remain engaged in dreaming.

Unfortunately, this divine gift of life does not get enough attention and nourishment from us. It is a rule of life that anything that gets attention from us becomes nourished. Lack of attention causes starvation. Pay attention to negativity and the negativity increases. Yes, it is important to work in life.

But there has to be a limit. We should leave aside all our doings and find some time to feel our being. In Zen they call it— sitting silently. There are certain things in life that we don't achieve with our doings; they happen by themselves. And that's why they are a gift.

Osho says: "Existence exists in order to exist. Our mind may not comprehend this because this belongs to the transcendental dimension."

OSHO FRAGRANCE

Nataraj: Non-duality of Dancer, the Dance

We often wonder about God: Where does he live? Does he really exist? This question has been bothering philosophers and common people alike since time immemorial.

Both Vedanta and Zen provide an appropriate answer to this question. They talk about non-duality in their own typical language. *Upanishads* say that God is not separate from the creation — creation and creativity are one. God is hidden in his creation as the dancer is in his dance. The Hindus define God as Nataraj; the dancer and the dance are inseparable.

Osho talks about the Nataraj meditation for God-realisation. He gives the example of one of the greatest dancers of this century: Nijinsky. There were some moments when Nijinsky would get so lost in his dance that everybody in the audience would feel that the dancer had disappeared. And then a miracle would happen: He would start jumping so high, a height that not even gravitation allows. And when he would start descending, he would come down slowly and gently like a feather.

Osho also tells a Zen story about a painter who was asked by an emperor to paint the Himalayas on his palace wall. The painter said he would need three years to do so. The emperor was astounded. "You will take three years?" he exclaimed.

235

"I have asked only for the minimum time because unless I become a part of the Himalayas I will not be able to paint them. I have to go and get lost in the Himalayas to paint a true picture of them," explained the painter.

After three years he returned and painted the wall in just three days. The emperor was awe-struck — he had never seen the Himalayas look so beautiful! He was so touched by their beauty that he found himself discovering little details in the painting. For instance, he said, "I can see a path winding around the mountains. Where does it go?"

To this the painter said, "Wait, let me go and see." Saying this, he disappeared into the painting and never returned. This is a perfect example of losing oneself in one's art. And it is another form of meditation.

Self-realisation is the Path to Bliss

We seem to pay too much importance to the opinions of other people because we don't know ourselves too well. This is because we don't have self-realisation. This is our main insecurity in psychological terms. We become extra touchy, sensitive and always defensive when we are attacked by other people and their opinions about us. Our whole identity and image is made by others. We remain in constant anxiety because others go on changing their opinions.

Osho says: "Opinions are like the climate: It is never the same. In the morning it was cloudy and now the clouds have gone. Now it is sunny, and the next moment it is raining. Opinions are just like clouds, just like the climate. This situation creates a vicious circle of misery. And the only way out is the self-realisation. How does a man of self-realisation act or behave in such situations?"

There's a very significant Zen story: A famous Zen Master, Hakuin was considered by his neighbours as one who led a pure life of a monk. One day it was discovered that a beautiful girl who lived near Hakuin's hut was pregnant. The parents of the girl were very angry. At first the girl would not say who the father was, but after much harassment she named Hakuin.

In great anger the parents went to Hakuin, but all he would say was, "Is that so?" After the child was born it was taken to Hakuin, who had lost his reputation by this time, although he didn't seem much disturbed by the fact. Hakuin took great care of the child. He obtained milk, food, and everything else the child needed from his neighbours.

A year later the young mother could not stand it any longer, so she told her parents the truth — the real father was a young man who worked in the fish market. The girl's parents went to Hakuin and told him the story, apologised at great length, asked his forgiveness and wanted to take the child back. The Master willingly gave the child and said, "Is that so?"

In his discourses on *No Water, No Moon*, Osho explains: "What must have happened inside Hakuin? Nothing! He simply listened to the fact that people had come to believe that he was the father, so he asked, 'Is that so?' That was all, that is all! He didn't react in any way — this way or that. He would not say yes, he would not say no. He was not defensive; he was open and vulnerable. Innocence is vulnerable; it is absolute vulnerability, openness. Whenever you defend, whenever you say that this is not so, you are afraid. Only fear is defensive. Fearlessness cannot be defensive. Fear always armours itself. One who knows himself is never disturbed by what you think about him."

Zen is about Living Now and Here

The Zen approach to life is very practical. It is not that of philosophy but meditation. Philosophy and meditation belong to opposite dimensions. Philosophy is basically meditation of the mind, while Zen belongs to the realm of no-mind or beyond mind.

Philosophy imagines the nature of reality while Zen experiences the reality directly. The reality is what is — or in words of J. Krishnamurti — that which is.

This reality is a direct perception of the present moment and living in the present moment — no past and no future. This is what a student of Zen in Japan learns from a Zen Master.

There is a significant story of a master of Zen who invited questions from his students. A student asked, "What future rewards can be expected by those who strive diligently with their lessons?"

Answered the Master, "Ask a question close to home."

A second student wanted to know, "How can I prevent my past follies from rising up to accuse me?"

The Master repeated, "Ask a question close to home."

A third student raised his hand to state, "Sir, we do not understand what is meant by asking a question close to home."

"To see far, first see near. Be mindful of the present moment, for it contains answers about future and past. What though just crossed your mind? Are you now sitting before me with a relaxed or with a tense physical body?

"Do I now have your full or partial attention? Close questions lead to distant answers."

This is exactly the Zen approach to life: Be here now!

Osho says that spiritual seeking is to be here and now, and you can only be here and now when there is no desiring mind. Just like a pendulum, the mind goes either to the past, in the memory, or to the future, in desires, in dreams. But it is never here and now; it always misses the point of here and now. We miss the reality between these waverings of past and future.

Reality is here and now. It is never past and never future; it is always present.

Now is the only moment. Now is the only time. It never passes. Now is eternal. It is always here, but we are not here. So to be a spiritual seeker means to be here. You may call it meditation, you may call it yoga, you may call it prayer. Whatever name is given, it makes no difference, the mind must not be.

And the mind exists only when there is a past or future, otherwise there is no mind.